Teacher Dialogical Self

Praise for *Teacher Dialogical Self: Professional development dynamics*

This book opens a new direction in understanding teachers' professional identity formation. It champions reflexivity within the teachers as they do their everyday work – their introspective feeling into what they are doing, their linking their own life course credos with their teacher role, and their humanity of working with young people who aspire towards new understandings – all these create a new perspective to our understanding the teaching profession. Impedovo has shown the value of the Dialogical Self Theory in making sense of teachers' professional development. Teaching is an art – a social theatrical performance that involves creative improvisation. This book is also a methodological innovation showing how autoethnography emerges as the main tool to study the professional development of teachers

—***Jaan Valsiner*, Foreign Member, Estonian Academy of Sciences**

Advances in Subjectivity and Development

Series Editor: Pablo Fossa

This series focuses on the processes of human development. Subjectivity, for its phenomenological approach to understanding human experience, and development, due to an emphasis on the transformative processes of psychological functions and its interaction with culture. This series is interested in topics such as cognitive development, educational processes, child, adolescent and adult development, socio-emotional development, relational processes, among others, all addressed through theoretical or empirical research

OTHER TITLES IN THE SERIES

Making Psychologist Training Meaningful in Higher Education
Subjectivity & Development in Rural Contexts
Humorous Actions, Play and Rules

Teacher Dialogical Self

Professional development dynamics

By

Maria Impedovo

Aix-Marseille Université, France

emerald PUBLISHING

United Kingdom – North America – Japan
India – Malaysia – China

Emerald Publishing Limited, Floor 5, Northspring, 21-23 Wellington Street, Leeds LS1 4DL

First edition 2026

Cover photo: istock and Shujun Chen

Reprints and permissions service
Contact: www.copyright.com

British Library Cataloguing in Publication Data
A catalogue record for this book is available from the British Library

ISBN: 978-1-80686-958-9 (Print hardback)
ISBN: 978-1-80686-960-2 (Print paperback)
ISBN: 978-1-80686-957-2 (PDF)
ISBN: 978-1-80686-959-6 (Epub)

Typeset by TNQ Tech

CONTENTS

ABOUT THE AUTHOR

Maria Impedovo is an Associate Professor in Educational Sciences at Aix-Marseille Université (France). Her research focuses on teacher education and professional development. With a background in both educational psychology and educational technology, she integrates qualitative and participatory methodologies in her work. She regularly publishes in the fields of cultural psychology, teacher identity, and educational innovation. https://orcid.org/0000-0003-2172-7105

INTRODUCTION

ABSTRACT

The growing complexity of teaching calls for renewed approaches to teacher education and professional development. Across 10 chapters, the book explores how lived experiences and dialogical positioning enable teachers to engage with multiple voices, construct new meanings, and develop their agency. Methodologically, the book combines autoethnographic reflection, teacher narratives, semiotic mediation, and art-based inquiry. Taken together, the book argues for teacher education that extends beyond technical competence, fostering spaces for self-exploration, dialogical engagement, and the cultivation of pedagogical presence.

Keywords: Professional development; lived experiences; autoethnographic reflection; teacher narratives; art-based inquiry

THEORETICAL FRAMEWORK

Given the growing complexity of teaching, it has become necessary to rethink teacher education and teacher professional development in ways that transcend purely technical or instrumental approaches and re/humanising education (Lyle, 2022). Today's educational demands require teachers who are capable of reflective practice, of adapting to diverse and changing conditions, and of engaging ethically with their profession into their (g)local context. Starting from the lived experiences (Vygotsky, 1978), the book explores deeply inside the spaces of positioning and negotiation of teacher identity positions (Hermans, 1996). This exploration invites teachers to engage with their own different voices, construct new meanings, and develop their agency (Wortham et al., 2017).

Teacher Dialogical Self, pages 1–10

doi:10.1108/978-1-80686-957-220261001

Professional Learning and Professional Development

The concept of professional development continues to hold a central place in educational research, particularly in the field of teaching and teacher-education. Yet, a closer examination of the literature reveals that many studies fail to clearly distinguish between two fundamentally different processes: (a) development, often understood in classical psychological theory as involving transformative, stage-like, or crisis-driven changes, and (b) learning, which generally refers to more gradual, cumulative forms of change (Vygotsky, 1986). Professional development is frequently reduced to the idea of progressive improvement in teaching practices, rather than being framed as a profound reconfiguration of the teacher's sense of self or professional identity. Vygotsky (1986) conceptualises development as a shift from one developmental stage to another process marked by reorganization. While within a given stage change may appear incremental and consistent, the transitions between stages are characterised by discontinuity and qualitative transformation. Within this framework, learning and development are interrelated yet distinct. Learning entails the acquisition of knowledge and skills through socially mediated interactions. It is embedded in communal practices and supported by cultural tools and shared activities. Development, on the other hand, involves a qualitative shift – a restructuring – that emerges, often unexpectedly, from ongoing learning processes (Vygotsky, 1986). This book invites a more nuanced and dynamic understanding of what it means to support teachers – not simply as learners acquiring new techniques, but as subjects undergo complex, sometimes unpredictable transformations over the course of their professional lives.

Professional Teacher Identity

Over the past 20 years, the notion of professional teacher identity has emerged as a central focus in educational research. A considerable body of literature highlights that teachers' ways of interpreting and engaging with their professional responsibilities are strongly intertwined with the development of their teacher identity (Beijaard et al., 2004). Scholars have highlighted that teachers' identities significantly shape how they engage with diverse educational contexts (Vähäsantanen et al., 2020). Put differently, the notion of professional identity is central, as it reflects the interplay of knowledge, competences, and dispositions through which teachers interpret their role and exercise agency in their practice.

Research has shown that professional teacher identity is closely linked to self-image, beliefs, and self-understanding (Chong & Low, 2009). It has also been described as a process of interpreting and negotiating personal, professional, and social relationships (Mahmoudi-Gahrouei et al., 2016). More recent perspectives emphasise identity as a dynamic construction shaped by experiences, cultural-historical contexts, and individual characteristics (Lamote & Engels, 2010). From a sociocultural standpoint (Vygotsky, 1978), teacher education entails not only developing competences but also engaging in identity formation, where meanings about self and profession are progressively built. Thus, professional identity can be understood both as a resource for making sense of one's role and as a cultural construct that defines expectations of being and acting as a teacher (Sachs, 2005).

From this perspective, teacher identity can be seen as a constructive process shaped by the diverse experiences teachers gain within their communities. These experiences reflect complex social interactions that are continuously interpreted and reinterpreted to form meanings about oneself and the teaching profession (Roth & Erstad, 2016). Individuals give structure to these experiences through 'voices', which articulate their position relative to the world and its objects (Bruner, 1990; Wortham, 2006). In doing so, these voices establish discursive stances and situate identity construction within temporal and spatial contexts, enabling the ongoing development of professional identity.

Development, therefore, is not simply about change, but about recognition of the self as becoming. In this process of becoming, the notion of agency – conceived as the capacity and readiness to act in relation to the demands of educational settings – emerges. Agency is not external to identity but rather constitutes one of its key expressions (Hökkä et al., 2017; Impedovo, 2016, 2021). The book invites us to investigate how subjective experiences – understood as discursive reconstructions of meaningful events – contribute simultaneously to shaping identity and the capacity to act.

Dialogical Self Framework: Applications and Insights

The book adopts broadly the Dialogical Self framework (Hermans, 2013; Hermans & Gieser, 2011). The self is emerging from the social, historical and societal process that transcend any individual -society dichotomy or separation (Hermans & Hermans-Konopka, 2010, p. 1).

It became a dynamic orchestration of the self's many voices (Bakhtin, 1986), held together in mutual resonance, creative tension, and ethical attention. Entering in a deep exploration of the teacher's subjective experiences, all the chapters in the book try to develop the question: *What does it mean to think the 'I'? And what happens when, thinking about it, we begin to hear its many voices, feel its tensions, and touch its ever-evolving form?*

In the following, the list of the 10 chapters of the book – also in Fig. 1.

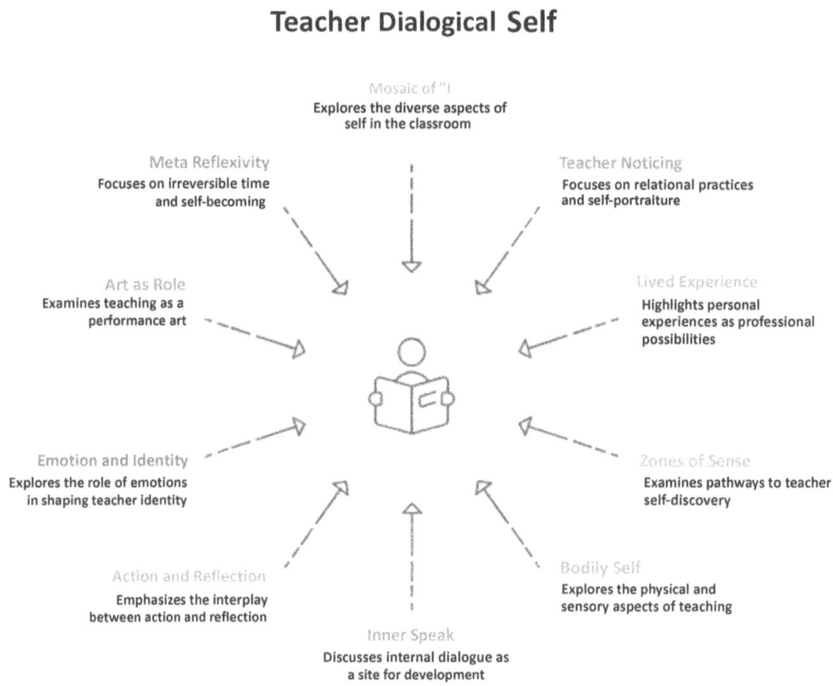

Fig. 1. Main Concepts in the Book.

- The Chapter 1 'The Mosaic of "I" into the classroom: Dialogical Intersectional Exploration' investigates the ways in which teacher educators' multifaceted identities through a dialogical and intersectional lens.
- The Chapter 2 'Teacher Noticing as Self-Portraiture: Relational Practices' questions how to shape inner professional life with the process of noticing, contributing in a regenerative way to their daily experience of teaching.
- The Chapter 3 'The Lived Experience as a Professional Possibility' explores the interplay of materiality and the dialogical self in shaping classroom pedagogy.
- The Chapter 4 'Zones of sense: Pathways to Teacher Self' explores the teacher's self-awareness by examining how sensory experiences – particularly with soundscapes and photographic images – can deepen pedagogical presence.
- The Chapter 5 'Exploring the Teacher bodily Self' examines how bodily movement, gesture, and posture serve not only as indicators

of internal emotional states but also as relational acts that shape pedagogical encounters.

- The Chapter 6 'Inner speak: Dwelling in Teacher professional development' explores the dynamic nature of inner speech through an autoethnographic lens.
- The Chapter 7 'The mutual feeding of action and reflection as a dialogical process' explores the mutual feeding of action and reflection in academic life through an autoethnographic approach to inner speech. This chapter offers a performative inquiry into the tensions, contradictions, and generative forces that shape scholarly becoming.
- The Chapter 8 'Emotion and Teacher Identity' explores the role of emotions – particularly negative emotions – in the professional life of teachers.
- The Chapter 9 'Art to be a teacher: a role to play' explores the metaphor of theatre as a framework for rethinking teacher identity, presence, and professional becoming. This approach calls for teacher education practices that support inner spectatorship, improvisational attention, and the poetic dimensions of pedagogical presence.
- The Chapter 10 'Teacher Reflexivity: Becoming in the irreversible time' explores teacher professional development through the lens of temporality. It argues that teaching and learning unfold within cyclical temporal patterns that shape both professional identity and pedagogical practice.

Two extra chapters close the book:

- Chapter 11: POINTS FOR DEBATE – The Act of Performing Teacher Professional Development and Wellbeing invites readers to consider how professional development can be enacted as a lived, embodied, and relational practice. It foregrounds the interplay between reflection, emotion, and action, exploring how teachers navigate the tensions between institutional expectations and personal growth, and how wellbeing can be fostered through ethically attentive and creative engagement with professional life.
- Chapter 12: POINTS FOR DEBATE – Writing Otherwise on Teacher Professional Identity turns attention to the possibilities of non-traditional academic writing. It presents writing as an experimental, imaginative, and playful practice, offering strategies for exploring the teacher Self in ways that disrupt conventional scholarly forms. Through alternative modalities – such as vignettes, artistic practices, metaphor, and performative reflection – the

chapter encourages both researchers and educators to reconsider how identity is represented, interrogated, and enacted in professional and academic contexts. Together, these concluding chapters emphasise the ethical, relational, and creative dimensions of teacher development and scholarship, leaving readers with questions, provocations, and invitations for further exploration.

Across its 10 chapters, the book portrays teacher identity as a dialogical and evolving process shaped by multiplicity, embodiment, emotion, and temporality. From the mosaic of intersecting selves to the subtle practices of noticing, inner speech, and reflection, the chapters highlight how sensory experiences, bodily presence, and emotional resonance contribute to becoming professional. Metaphors of theatre and cyclical time further expand this perspective, showing teaching as a performative, situated, and rhythmic practice. Taken together, the book argues for teacher education that goes beyond technical skills, creating spaces for self-exploration, relational awareness, and the cultivation of pedagogical presence.

The Fil Rouge of 'as if' Tension

According to Valsiner (2005), the root idea of scaffolding – guidance – entails purposefulness of the actor and the directional nature of the act. The notion of scaffolding is outlined in terms of semiotic mechanisms that regulate the temporal re-organisation within the structure of Dialogical Self.

The 'as if' tension reassumes this provisional quality – neither fully real nor entirely false – that creates a dynamic tension generative of professional development growth. This anticipatory orientation, which might be described as a 'future anterior' stance, underpins a developmental process in which the imagined future casts its light backward, influencing present choices, motivations, and forms of participation. The 'as if' modality creates a psychological tension: between what is and what could be, grounded in the active projection of meaning and potential. In this view, acting 'as if' presupposes the existence of a guiding image of the self – not necessarily explicit or fully articulated, but sufficiently present to generate intentional movement. Development becomes the name for a specific kind of tension: between what one currently embodies and what one is moving towards as if it were already true. For example, a novice teacher may begin to act 'as if' they are already capable of sustaining inclusive pedagogy, even before mastery has been achieved. This form of anticipatory embodiment is not merely performative but transformational – it allows the future to become operative in the present, shaping perception, affect, and action in profound ways. The 'as if' tension is thus not reducible to aspiration or goal setting; it is affectively and existentially charged. It holds the potential to reorganise one's internal hierarchy of values and I-positions (Hermans, 2013; Hermans & Gieser, 2011), allowing emergent positions of the self to gain ascendancy over habitual, inherited ones. In Dialogical Self Theory, this could be understood as the moment when a future-oriented I-position ('I as a competent teacher') begins to exert influence on the system, challenging older, more static self-definitions ('I as uncertain' or 'I as a beginner').

METHODOLOGY

Auto-Ethnographic Data, Teaching and Academic Experience

This book draws mainly on autoethnographic material grounded in both my academic experiences – mainly in a 10 years' experience as teacher educators. This is related to: Chapters 1; 2; 3; 4; 5; 6; 7; and 10.

Autoethnography, as a qualitative research approach, offers a means for researchers to narrate their lived experiences within a context they inhabit, producing a situated account. Such self-reflexive inquiry, as Dauphinee (2010) notes, opens the possibility of engaging with aspects of us – and of others – that often remain unseen.

Autoethnography enables the researcher to interrogate, disrupt, and reframe their own perception of reality, thus making visible the social, cultural, ethical, and political forces that shape it (Ellis et al., 2011). In this process, feelings long concealed, motivations overlooked, and emotions pushed aside (Canagarajah, 2012) emerge, contributing to a form of knowledge rooted in one's positionality and identity (Anderson, 2006).

My approach moved along the spectrum between evocative and analytic autoethnography (Allen-Collinson, 2013), seeking to capture the personal meanings of experiences.

Given that 'in the process of writing about ourselves, we also write about others' (Sparkes, 2013, p. 207). In this spirit, I anonymised all references to students, colleagues, and the institution.

As with other forms of qualitative inquiry, the aim is neither to produce quantifiable outcomes nor to generalise. The validity and trustworthiness of this self-study lie in its capacity to resonate with readers, evoking a sense that the experiences described are authentic, credible, and conceivable (Ellis et al., 2011). To achieve this, I draw on a range of narrative accounts – vignettes (Schratz et al., 2013) and reflective accounts (Saldaña, 2016).

Complementary Set of Data: Teacher Narrative Accounts

As a complementary set of data, some of the narrative accounts draw on teacher education sessions conducted to enhance teaching practices analysis and research project collaborations analysing teaching emotions

(Denzin, 2006; Doecke et al., 2000). As data collection, teachers were invited to recount brief lived experiences (vignette, anecdotes, narrative accounts) from their professional lives – instances in which emotions, interactions, and self-perceptions were especially salient. This is related to: Chapters 8 and 9.

Semiotic Mediation and Art-Based Inquiry

The concept of the sign underscores its mediating role in human activity. Mediation through signs reveals that human life is a continuous, open-ended process: it signifies the present moment while simultaneously reaching beyond it. Signs enable human beings to act, play, influence, simulate, imitate, experiment, and learn. They form the core of what Valsiner (2014, 2021) describes as semiotic mediation – a universal process through which human experience takes shape. In the human psyche, this mediation is far more than a mere representation of the external world or the static use of symbolic forms. Rather, it unfolds as a dynamic, recursive movement across diverse sign systems and relational processes, generating experiences that are creative, subjective, and shared (Impedovo, 2025). By mobilising a vast repertoire of signs – ranging from gestures and language to artefacts and symbolic practices – people engage in activities such as playing, performing, simulating, and imagining (Valsiner, 2020). Cultural practices like play, literature, and theatrical performance enact this semiotic function in its purest form by invoking the 'as if' dimension – the human capacity to conceive fictional scenarios, envision possible worlds, and anticipate future realities (Valsiner, 2021). In this spirit, the book draws on artistic and cultural expressions – portraits, myths, sculptures, performances, and acts of play – not simply as illustrations, but as openings into alternative ways of connecting with broader social and cultural productions across different times and spaces.

CONCLUSION

By bridging theory and practice, this book serves as a resource for those seeking to navigate the complexities of teaching and to foster an agentive stance. It offers an intimate exploration of teacher identity, delving into the intricate interplay between personal understanding and professional dimensions. By providing a deep, reflective perspective on how internal experiences – such as emotions, self-awareness, and inner dialogue - shape and are shaped by the teaching role, it seeks to enhance overall effectiveness and well-being within the educational environment. The final contribution is to sensibilise teachers with a nuanced understanding of our identities, enabling them to navigate their roles with greater authenticity and resilience. Through this introspective journey, the book aspires to foster a more supportive, engaged, and balanced teaching practice that benefits both teachers and their students.

REFERENCES

Allen-Collinson, J. (2013). Autoethnography as the engagement of self/other, self/culture, self/politics, selves/futures. In *Handbook of autoethnography* (pp. 281–299). Ashgate.

Anderson, L. (2006). Analytic autoethnography. *Journal of Contemporary Ethnography, 35*(4), 373–395.

Bakhtin, M. (1986). *Speech genres and other late essays.* University of Texas Press.

Beijaard, D., Meijer, P. C., & Verloop, N. (2004). Reconsidering research on teachers' professional identity. *Teaching and Teacher Education, 20,* 107–128. https://doi.org/10.1016/j.tate.2003.07.001

Bruner, J. (1990). *Acts of meaning.* Harvard University Press.

Canagarajah, A. S. (2012). Teacher development in a global profession: An autoethnography. *TESOL quarterly, 46*(2), 258–279.

Chong, S., & Low, E. (2009). Why I want to teach and how I feel about teaching—Formation of teacher identity from pre-service to the beginning teacher phase. *Educational Research for Policy and Practice, 8*(1), 59. https://doi.org/10.1007/s10671-008-9056-z

Dauphinee, E. (2010). The ethics of autoethnography. *Review of International Studies, 36*(3), 799–818.

Denzin, N. K. (2006). *Analytic autoethnography, or déjà vu all over again* (4, pp. 419–428.

Doecke, B., Brown, J., & Loughran, J. (2000). Teacher talk: The role of story and anecdote in constructing professional knowledge for beginning teachers. *Teaching and Teacher Education, 16*(3), 335–348.

Ellis, C., Adams, T. E., & Bochner, A. P. (2011). Autoethnography: An overview. *Historical Social Research,* 273–290.

Hermans, H. J. (1996). Voicing the self: From information processing to dialogical interchange. *Psychological Bulletin, 119*(1), 31. https://doi.org/10.1037/0033-2909.119.1.31

Hermans, H. J. M. (2013). The dialogical self in education: Introduction. *Journal of Constructivist Psychology, 26*(2), 81–89. https://doi.org/10.1080/10720537.2013.759018

Hermans, H. J., & Gieser, T. (Eds.). (2011). *Handbook of dialogical self theory.* Cambridge University Press.

Hermans, H. J. M., & Hermans-Konopka, A. (2010). *Dialogical self theory: Positioning and counter-positioning in a globalizing society.* Cambridge University Press.

Hökkä, P., Vähäsantanen, K., & Mahlakaarto, S. (2017). Teacher educators' collective professional agency and identity – Transforming marginality to strength. *Teaching and Teacher Education, 63,* 36–46. https://doi.org/10.1016/j.tate.2016.12.001

Impedovo, M. (2025). Mirroring the self through Hamlet affective aesthetic experience. *Integrative Psychological and Behavioral Science, 59*(3), 1–16.

Impedovo, M. A. (2016). In-service teachers' sense of agency after participation in a research master course. *International Journal of Educational Psychology, 5*(3), 281–307.

Impedovo, M. A. (2021). *Identity and teacher professional development: A reflective, collaborative and agentive learning journey.* SPRINGER BRIEF. ISBN 978-3-030-71367-6. ISBN online 978-3-030-71366-9. https://link.springer.com/book/10.1007/978-3-030-71367-6

Lamote, C., & Engels, N. (2010). The development of student teachers' professional identity. *European Journal of Teacher Education, 33*(1), 3–18. https://doi.org/10.1080/02619760903457735

Lyle, E. (Ed.). (2022). *Re/humanizing education.* Brill.

Mahmoudi-Gahrouei, V., Tavakoli, M., & Hamman, D. (2016). Understanding what is possible across a career: Professional identity development beyond transition to teaching. *Asia Pacific Education Review, 17*(4), 581–597. https://doi.org/10.1007/s12564-016-9457-2

Roth, S., & Erstad, O. (2016). Positional identities in educational transitions: Connecting con temporary and future trajectories among multiethnic girls. *Ethnography and Education, 11*(1), 57–73. https://doi.org/10.1080/17457823.2015.1040044

Sachs, J. (2005). Teacher education and the development of professional identity: Learning to be a teacher. In P. Denicolo & M. Kopf (Eds.), *Connecting policy and practice: Challenges for teaching and learning in schools and universities* (pp. 2–21). Psychology Press.

Saldaña, J. (2016). *Ethnotheatre: Research from page to stage.* Routledge.

Schratz, M., Schwarz, J. F., & Westfall-Greiter, T. (2013). Looking at two sides of the same coin: Phenomenologically oriented vignette research and its implications for teaching and learning. *Studia paedagogica, 18*(4), 57–73.

Sparkes, A. C. (2013). Autoethnography at the will of the body: Reflections on a failure to produce on time. In *Contemporary British autoethnography* (pp. 203–211). Sense Publishers.

Vähäsantanen, K., Paloniemi, S., Räikkönen, E., & Hökkä, P. (2020). Professional agency in a university context: Academic freedom and fetters. *Teaching and Teacher Education, 89*, 103000. https://doi.org/10.1016/j.tate.2019.103000

Valsiner, J. (2005). Scaffolding within the structure of dialogical self: Hierarchical dynamics of semiotic mediation. *New Ideas in Psychology, 23*(3), 197–206.

Valsiner, J. (2014). *An invitation to cultural psychology.* Sage.

Valsiner, J. (2020). *Sensuality in human living: The cultural psychology of affect.* Springer.

Valsiner, J. (2021). *General human psychology: Foundations for a science.* Springer.

Vygotsky, L. S. (1978). *Mind in society: Development of higher psychological processes.* Harvard University Press.

Vygotsky, L. S. (1986). *Thought and language.* MIT Press.

Wortham, S. (2006). *Learning identity: The joint emergence of social identification and academic learning.* Cambridge University Press.

Wortham, S., Kim, D., & May, S. (Eds.). (2017). *Discourse and education.* Springer.

CHAPTER 1

THE MOSAIC OF 'I' INTO THE CLASSROOM: DIALOGICAL INTERSECTIONAL EXPLORATION

ABSTRACT

This chapter explores the ways in which teachers' multifaceted identities through a dialogical and intersectional lens. Drawing on the Dialogical Self-Theory, the study conceptualises the teacher self as composed of multiple, interacting positions that emerge and negotiate meaning within situated contexts. Integrating intersectionality as a critical framework, this chapter foregrounds how axes of identity such as class and gender interact dynamically in educational settings, producing both tensions and possibilities. The methodology is grounded in reflexive narrative and autoethnographic inquiry, expressed in vignettes, to uncover how a meta-abstracted position emerges from the interplay of positions.

Keywords: Dialogical self; intersectionality; class; gender; tensions; meta-abstracted position

Teacher Dialogical Self, pages 11–24

doi:10.1108/978-1-80686-957-220261002

INTRODUCTION

This autoethnographic study explores a personal journey as a teacher educator through the lens of reflexivity and of the Dialogical Self-Theory (DST), understood as a relational stance. Starting from the idea of reflexivity as the ability to question the multiplicity of yourself as you question others, this inquiry seeks to map some position inherent in the professional identity and practice of those who prepare others to teach. Autoethnography, as both method and mode of knowledge production, enables a situated and embodied account of professional development. Through narrative and critical self-examination, I position myself within the overlapping spheres of personal experience, institutional structures, and pedagogical responsibility. Reflexivity here is not a solitary act of self-awareness, but an ethical orientation towards becoming-with others – with students, with colleagues, and with the broader educational community. This study embraces the vulnerability of seeing the multiplicity of yourself – acknowledging the contradictions, emotions, and power relations that shape professional development. It is in this shared space of inquiry and reciprocity that the 'I' of the teacher educator begins to move towards a collective 'we'. This reflection contributes to the growing scholarship on teacher educators' reflexive practices by offering a lived account of how professional knowledge and identity are constructed through recursive engagement with self and context. It calls for a reconceptualisation of professional development as an ongoing, relational, and ethical process – one that embraces the uncertainty of becoming. The chapter is organised as follows: The first section opens with a discussion on Self and Sensemaking within the changing landscape of academia. This is followed by an exploration of the theoretical framework of DST as applied to teachers' professional identity. The inquiry – both deeply personal and socially situated – is illustrated through two examples of intersectional selves. The first focuses on the identity of first-generation scholars and working-class academics, while the second examines the performance of academic identity in the context of conferences. The chapter concludes highlighting the role of openness to contradiction and novelty.

SELF AND SENSEMAKING IN THE CHANGING ACADEMIA

In the context of polycrisis (Albert, 2024; Roberts, 2024), higher education institutions are confronted with rapidly evolving demands, uncertainties, and transnational challenges that directly impact the academic self (Aarrevaara & Dobson, 2013). Academic staff are not merely actors within institutional structures; they are also individuals engaged in an ongoing process of sensemaking (Weick & Weick, 1995), in which personal identity, professional values, and contextual realities intertwine. In the changing landscape of academia, the self is shaped by overlapping pressures: the globalisation of education (Altbach, 2016), demands for intercultural competence (Deardorff, 2006), and the increasing precarity and fragmentation of academic work (Gill, 2014). The raising of neoliberalism, requiring teachers and academics to navigate complex socio-cultural and institutional terrains while maintaining coherence in their professional identity (Becher & Trowler, 2001; Brooks et al., 2020). Sensemaking becomes not only a cognitive process but also an emotional and ethical engagement with the demands of collaborative, transnational work. The autoethnographic perspective offers a valuable lens here, enabling academics to critically reflect on their lived experiences, the negotiation of cultural capital (Bochner & Ellis, 2022), and the reconfiguration of professional habits in light of new global realities (Marginson & Rhoades, 2002). Ultimately, the transformation of academia under polycrisis conditions is not solely an organizational challenge; it is also a deeply personal journey of making sense of shifting roles, values, and meanings (Anderson et al., 2020).

THEORETICAL FRAMEWORK

According to DST, identity can be understood as composed of multiple self-positions, each offering a distinct perspective (Hermans, 2013). A self-position represents a particular voice that has been internalized in the presentation of the self. Drawing from Bakhtin's ideas (1994), such a voice can be conceptualised as 'a speaking personality' that offers a specific worldview. The dialogical self is not reducible to a series of isolated, internal traits or monological features. Rather, it should be understood in relation to other positions and coalitions of positions that co-exist within the self.

The dialogical self is always situated – tied to roles (e.g., self-as-teacher, self-as-mother), embedded in time and space. Yet, it is also fluid and capable of shifting from one position to another depending on contextual changes (Hermans & Gieser, 2011).

This perspective is particularly helpful in highlighting the discontinuous, diverse, and socially constructed nature of identity, suggesting a flexible self-composed of multiple positions that reflect different facets of one's subjectivity. These self-positions are dynamically relational, shaped at the intersection of personal and societal forces through tension (Impedovo, 2022). Moreover, they are inherently social, arising in interactions between individuals and groups (Impedovo & Ligorio, 2025).

Concepts such as uncertainty and discontinuity depict identity as fluid and in constant motion – shifting across contexts and moments. Yet, over time, some self-positions may become more rigid or 'crystallised'. The self can oscillate between different – even opposing – positions (both internal and between self and perceived or imagined others). Each position carries its own voice, allowing for dialogical relations, negotiations, agreements or disagreements, and potential integrations within the self (Hermans & Gieser, 2011). Thus, the dialogical self includes not only internal self-positions that reflect aspects of one's identity, but also external positions that represent the perspectives of others.

These external positions often correspond to the imagined voices of significant others and are involved in processes of negotiation and dialogue with internal self-positions. External others may also represent institutional or cultural voices – such as those of traditions, ideologies, or values (Grossen & Muller Mirza, 2020). The influence of these voices may manifest through real interpersonal dialogue (external dialogue) or through inner dialogue, in which internal and external self-positions interact in imagined conversation (Fossa, 2022).

Individuals frequently experience tension between different self-positions, both internal and external. These tensions may produce feelings of discomfort, vulnerability, or even a sense of being overwhelmed. As Monereo and Hermans (2023, p. 454) observe, it is important to 'acknowledge one's own contradictions and revisit the self-positions that give rise to tensions, fears, and anxieties in order to transcend and harmonise them'. Valsiner's theory of the dialogical self conceptualises identity as a dynamic system of 'I-positions' organised hierarchically yet constantly restructured through lived tensions. Central to this framework is the idea that the self evolves through the *emergence of abstracted positions* – meta-perspectives born from contradiction, emotional conflict, and relational dialogue. The tension between roles (e.g., being a mother and an academic, or an emigrant and a national institutional actor) does not fragment the self but acts as a catalyst for higher-order synthesis. These synthesised, abstracted positions serve not to resolve tension but to hold it in creative suspension, allowing for new professional meanings to emerge.

Several interesting publications have focused on teacher identity from a dialogical perspective (Arvaja, 2024). For example, Stenberg and Maaranen (2020) focus on the teacher's identity relationships with the I-positions in the didactic triangle. When teachers reflect on their past and present experiences that hold personal significance, they can become aware of their often-implicit sub-identities and discover which sub-identities are relevant in this specific context. Exploring the relationship between different I-positions helps to overcome ambivalence and supports future teachers in creating a coalition of different positions (Konopka et al., 2018). However, the power of self-narratives lies not only in their ability to seek out and represent coherent identities but also in their capacity to express and manage multiple fragmented and partly conflicting selves while offering several scenarios for the self (Wortham, 2001).

METHODOLOGY

This study adopts an autoethnographic approach, grounded in experience as a teacher educator. Autoethnography, as a qualitative research methodology, offers a textured and situated way of accessing self-in-context – where the 'self' is not treated as an isolated entity, but as fundamentally emergent within historical, societal, and cultural processes that dissolve the dichotomy between individual and society (Hermans & Hermans-Konopka, 2010). Rather than merely recounting personal narrative, autoethnography enables a reflexive inquiry that contests and interrogates the social structures, professional expectations, and political tensions that frame identity. It foregrounds the blurred boundary between the personnel and the public, where knowledge is shaped by location, embodiment, and the multiplicity of lived roles (Bochner & Ellis, 2022). As such, the self-explored here is not static or internally coherent but dialogical and dynamic formed in tension with others, institutions, ideologies, and internal multiplicity. Drawing from Valsiner's model, I understand this self as composed of multiple 'I-positions', each activated contexts and negotiated within a hierarchical system of meaning. The emergence of new, abstracted I-positions – particularly through professional and existential tension – represents a central concern of this inquiry. By beginning with the 'auto', I reflect on my personal and professional journey from the standpoint of the present, tracing how body-world-processes (Blackman, 2012) – material, emotional, cultural, and institutional – have constrained or enabled my becoming. These reflections are not merely evocative but also analytic (Allen-Collinson, 2013), as I move along the continuum of personal meaning-making and structural critique. The aim is to understand how my practice has been shaped by, and in turn attempts to shape, the wider ethical and political landscape of teacher education. In this process, 'hidden feelings, forgotten motivations, and suppressed emotions' (Canagarajah, 2012, p. 261) are not incidental but central – they reveal the underlying currents of identity work and professional positioning. Through this methodological lens, my inquiry becomes both deeply personal and socially anchored.

Metaphors of Embodied Complexity

To access and express this complex dialogical self, I have chosen to structure the autoethnographic narrative around the symbolism of the Hindu cosmology. This metaphorical device – specifically, the reference to the avatars – allows me to articulate the intersectional, transformative, and situational nature of my identity as a teacher educator. In Hindu philosophy, the deity avatars represent interventions across time to restore balance and protect cosmic order. These symbolic avatars are not fixed roles but contextual responses – symbolic of the tensions I experienced and the developmental syntheses that emerged through them. Metaphorically, these avatars can serve as a narrative scaffold to understand the transformational journey of the teacher educator, especially when lived through the lens of intersectionality and reflexivity. My lived identity crosses multiple axes – woman, teacher educator, researcher, emigrant, psychologist, and more. Each intersectional position is not simply additive but relationally transformative, much like each avatar reveals a different mode of action. Below, I reframe two examples of intersectional selves in dialogue with the avatars, as symbolic expressions of evolving pedagogical being – at the intersection of institutional expectations, professional responsibility, and ethical commitment to learner development. The first example is about first-generation scholars and Working-Class Academics identity, and the second example uses a vignette (Schratz et al., 2013) about the performance of academic identity in the context of the conference.

Swimming Without a Map: First-Generation Scholar as Embodied Knowledge

In the following section, I repost my contribution in an editorial special issue (Markides et al., 2021, p. 6).

> *'My culture is that of the South of Italy: historically more rural, isolated, and poor than the North of Italy. A history of farmers, laborers, woodcutters, as well expressed in the title book "Formiche di Puglia" (The ants of Puglia) of the local author Tommaso Fiore (1951): the ants are the peasants, the workers of the countryside, the starving. The dignity and the daily works of the so-called "I cafoni" – the rough people working the earth and the stone - today attract tourists into the white and clean streets of Puglia. Valuing the diversity of intelligence and different forms of knowledge remains a modern challenge. I entered into the education world as a separate reality from mine, assuming the complex social role of "the student." Staying in the educational system helps me bridge cultural and social gaps, overcoming monological perspectives and representations.*
>
> *Today, as a teacher-educator, I search for dialogic and collaborative possibilities between fields, territories, subjects, social status, cultural and racial artificial separations. Multiple wayfinding conversations are possible to be opened through education, so I repeat to myself: "I must always remember that the real leap is to bring the invention into existence. In the world I travel to, I create myself endlessly" (Franz Fanon, 1967)'.*

Like the mythic avatar in Hindu philosophy who dives into uncharted waters to preserve knowledge, the first-generation student enters the world of academia without inherited maps, navigating currents not originally designed for them. My own academic journey began from a position of economic precarity – raised in a low-income household where cultural and educational capital were not readily available. Yet, a persistent curiosity for learning and a desire to grow beyond social boundaries marked my path early on. Growing up, I was constantly seeking opportunities for cultural and intellectual stimulation, often outside formal schooling. Completing my doctoral studies in Italy became not an endpoint but a transition – a moment that coincided with the need to emigrate abroad. This trajectory shaped my fundamental belief in education for personal and collective transformation (Giroux, 1993). My engagement with critical literature – such as emancipatory pedagogy and the writings of Frantz Fanon (Impedovo & Ferreira-Meyers, 2021) – has been collected and shared through academic publications and reflective blogs. A pivotal moment in deepening my understanding of my first-generation scholar identity came in July 2021, when I presented at the Working-Class Academics Conference, 'a conference by and for working-class academics.' This experience catalysed a broader reflection on the tensions I have encountered throughout my academic career.

The literature on working-class academics frequently draws on personal narratives and metaphoric language to confront the emotional and structural challenges of academic life. Concepts such as being a 'ghost' in the university (Cruz, 2021) or the 'punkademic' (Furness, 2012) express a do-it-yourself ethic, a passionate frustration, and a refusal to silence discomfort. These metaphors articulate an affective landscape marked by imposter syndrome, alienation, lack of cultural capital, and micro-aggressions (Warnock, 2016). Class, as both a sociological and experiential category, has been extensively studied through its psychological, professional, and embodied effects. Scholars have described feelings of shame (Lee, 2017), embarrassment (Case, 2017), class-based neurosis (de Gaulejac, 2016), and the imposter phenomenon (Friedman, 2016). What these studies ask – and what my experience echoes – is how working-class identities shape scholarly practice and how this positioning can contribute to a more inclusive and transformative pedagogy. The academic space itself is codified through middle-class sensibilities: through speech, dress, posture, and unspoken expectations. For those from working-class backgrounds, encountering this dominant habitus can produce feelings of inauthenticity and dislocation. One becomes suspended in a liminal space (De Luca Picione, 2021), neither fully belonging to the culture of origin nor completely assimilated into the world of academia. To swim in these waters as a first-generation scholar is to continuously negotiate between inherited histories and professional expectations, personal authenticity and institutional legitimacy. And yet, it is precisely in this in-betweenness that critical consciousness can emerge – a space where one learns not only to survive, but also to name and reshape the currents themselves.

As a teacher educator working in a country where I had not received formal schooling, I was often met with unsettling emotions – particularly when I was unfamiliar with references or practices commonly shared by my students. I had to adapt quickly by listening attentively and seeking information to understand the educational system. These experiences, although uncomfortable, gave rise to critical emotional self-inquiry (Zembylas &

Papamichael, 2017). Emotions, like discomfort, rather than being an obstacle, opens up space for questioning dominant norms and invites the re-examination of inherited beliefs and power structures. For example, what Cruz (2021, p. 133) refers to as a 'working-class pedagogy' signals an innovative approach to teaching – one that raises resilience, adaptability, and critical insight shaped by working-class experience.

Focussing on my own identity has enabled me to more clearly articulate the multiple positions I occupy – as woman, migrant, scholar – and to see how these intersect in complex, often conflicting ways. This internal work of alignment and harmonisation is not always visible, but it is essential. The emotional, social, and experiential history of both educators and learners should be recognised as epistemological and professional resources. Past and present lived experiences are still under-recognised and undervalued in education, despite their critical role in shaping perspective and fostering agency.

The Performance of Academic Identity in the Conference

In the following, I use a vignette – collected in the last academic year from my experience as a teacher educator – to bring one example of lived experience.

> *As soon as I wake up in the morning, the thoughts come automatically.*
>
> *Everything I have to do during the day rushes in at once: the fast pace of time, the call to a relative I shouldn't forget, the message I need to send to a colleague about a last-minute substitution; and, above all the tasks to do, the presentation for the conference... The thoughts take up all the mental space but the tensions for the formal presentation are more into the stomach. Somehow, I find myself already in the kitchen, making coffee – dressed and ready, though I don't remember choosing my clothes. My body moved through the routine before my mind caught up.*
>
> *I try to decide the right attitude for the presentation: I recognise it is important to share and open the discussions, accept to be questioned, but sometimes I have the impression that one performance brings a judgement on the whole career: is it fair?*
>
> *I know that the oscillation between willing to share and feat to be judged will go on as a pendulum: it will stop during the presentation, when I will be involved in the action.*

Like the mythic avatar that goes beyond binary limitations – neither inside nor outside, also teachers and academics are invited to go beyond traditional divisions. As a woman in academia, I am sensible to assert presence in spaces where power and legitimacy are still gendered.

Over time, academic conferences have become critical sites for constructing and legitimising scholarly identity (Folabit & Jita, 2024). Historically, one can trace the itinerant nature of academic exchange to the *clerici vagantes* – wandering scholars of the mediaeval period, including students and professors who travelled from city to city in search of knowledge and intellectual adventure. These figures contributed significantly to the literary atmosphere of the so-called 12th-century Renaissance, producing vibrant Latin poetry and fostering a sense of translocal academic community (Henderson & Moreau, 2019).

Despite ongoing efforts towards equity, power and legitimacy in academia remain deeply gendered constructs (Biggs et al., 2018). Indeed, in contemporary academia, however, the conference space continues to reflect structural inequalities, particularly for women (Anderson et al., 2019). Furthermore, for women with family responsibilities or caregiving roles, practical barriers – such as travel logistics or childcare – further restrict their access to these important professional forums (Timperley et al., 2020). These constraints can evoke feelings of vulnerability (Aiston & Fo, 2020). The cumulative effect of these constraints is what Lendák-Kabók (2020) terms an 'academic nemesis': a system of symbolic regulation and surveillance that confines women to peripheral roles and silences their participation. In response, many female academics engage in what Humphreys and Brown (2017) conceptualise as *identity work* – strategic self-presentation and discursive practices aimed at securing recognition and legitimacy within academic communities. While these practices may sustain a professional presence, they often fail to align with personal fulfilment or authentic scholarly engagement (Folabit & Jita, 2024).

Thus, conferences can become performative spaces where gendered power dynamics are enacted, challenged, or internalised through the ongoing negotiation of academic identity.

DISCUSSION: *REFLEXIVE BECOMING*

Hermans and Hermans-Konopka (2010, p. 1) argue that 'the self is not considered as an entity in itself but rather as emerging from social, historical, and societal processes that transcend any individual-society dichotomy or separation'. My identity as a teacher educator does not develop in isolation; it is co-constructed through dialogs with institutional histories, cultural norms, family legacies, and collective narratives of education.

As seen before, my positioning as a first-generation student is entangled with broader socio-economic and historical movements around access to education. Similarly, my experience as an emigrant is embedded in geopolitical patterns of mobility and belonging. Even my pedagogical practices are shaped by inherited and contested models of what it means to teach, to lead, and to care. Each I-position I embody is, therefore, inherently relational, not only in terms of interpersonal interaction but also as a product of the wider symbolic, historical, and institutional ecology.

This understanding resituates reflexivity not merely as a personal exercise but as a deeply situated act – one that recognises the self as both agent and product of the social world. Through this lens, the dialogical self becomes a site where personal and societal narratives intersect, where individual becoming is always already collective. Each position enables understanding as a *response* to particular socio-cultural and institutional challenges.

Each role emerges, like the avatars, in moments of disequilibrium and transformation. Reflexivity, then, is the connective tissue – the capacity to see across these layers. This approach stresses the multi-dimensionality of being a teacher educator but also situates intersectionality as an evolving praxis – one that bridges the autobiographical and the collective.

Intersectionality, traditionally used to analyse overlapping systems of oppression, can also be re-read through a dialogical lens as a structure of internal multiplicity. These positions do not exist in isolation but in relational clusters that speak to each other, negotiate, compete, and sometimes conflict. These positions are not additive; they interact dynamically, shaping and being shaped by one another through situated dialogue.

The internal dynamics of the self often involve struggles between assumed positions – tensions between how one sees oneself and how one is perceived or expected to perform. These struggles are not merely intrapsychic but are shaped by external discourses and social expectations: a teacher educator might experience conflict between being an innovator and being perceived as too idealistic. These tensions generate zones of dissonance, but also spaces of emergence. As Valsiner (2014) suggests, such tensions can give rise to new, abstracted self-positions that go beyond existing binaries, allowing the subject to move towards a dialectical synthesis rather than a simple resolution. In this process, reflexivity becomes central – not as a form of introspective closure, but as a dialogical opening towards complexity. Identity work, therefore, is also ethical work: it requires navigating contradiction, embracing dissonance, and sustaining dialogue among the voices that make up the self, in his or her self-continuity (Uriko, 2019).

Reflexivity, as conceptualised here, functions both as a method and a stance. It orchestras a dialogical interplay, allowing me to move from a fragmented understanding of professional identity towards a dialectical synthesis. This synthesis does not dissolve differences but integrates it into a more complex self-system. Each I-position, activated by real-life tensions, contributes to the emergence of a more abstracted and integrated self. Such abstract syntheses represent moments of transformation within the self, made possible through openness to contradiction and novelty (Valsiner, 2014).

CONCLUSION

To stay inside the same register of Hinduism, the visual metaphor of the composite elephant offers support for anchoring. In this style, painted representations of different animals or animals and humans are combined to form a larger image within the painting. Each figure within the elephant represents a metaphor for a distinct element of experience or voice within the self: yet together they form a coherent, recognisable (abstract) whole. In the example in Fig. 2, a group of women playing music with different instruments are combined to form a purple elephant.

Fig. 2. Composite Elephant – Deccan Painting – Early 17th Century. *Source:* (Natasha Khaitan, CC BY-SA 4.0 https://creativecommons.org/licenses/by-sa/4.0, via Wikimedia Commons) https://commons.wikimedia.org/wiki/File:Composite_Elephant_-_Deccan_Painting_-_Early_17th_century.jpg. This file is licenced under the Creative Commons Attribution-Share Alike 4.0 International licence.

Similarly, from an intersectional perspective, the image embodies the idea that identity emerges at the crossroads of multiple categories – such as gender, class, ethnicity, and professional role – none of which can be understood in isolation. The elephant, a traditional symbol of memory and wisdom, here becomes a living archive of lived experiences, affective intensities, and positionalities. The composite form reflects the complexity of subjectivity, where apparent contradictions coexist in layered harmony. It also evokes the pedagogical imperative of acknowledging this inner diversity in the classroom: to teach from the whole self, and to meet others as equally complex and multifaceted beings.

If we are to cultivate harmonious I-positions in individuals and groups (von Fircks, 2024), we should acknowledge the affective and ethical dimensions of identity, the hierarchical interplay of self-positions, and the struggle for coherence across intersecting lines of experience. Intersectionality can thus be understood not only as a socio-political framework, but also as psychological grammar for negotiating inner diversity.

REFERENCES

Aarrevaara, T., & Dobson, I. (2013). Movers and shakers: Do academics control their own work? In *The work situation of the academic profession in Europe: Findings of a survey in twelve countries* (pp. 159–181). Springer Netherlands.

Aiston, S. J., & Fo, C. K. (2020). The silence/ing of academic women. *Gender and Education, 33*(2), 138–155. https://doi.org/10.1080/09540253.2020.1716955

Albert, M. J. (2024). *Navigating the polycrisis: Mapping the futures of capitalism and the Earth.* MIT Press.

Altbach, P. G. (2016). *Global perspectives on higher education* (p. 303). Johns Hopkins University Press.

Allen-Collinson, J. (2013). Autoethnography as the engagement of self/other, self/culture, self/politics, selves/futures. *Handbook of Autoethnography*, 281–299.

Anderson, J., Goodall, H., & Trahar, S. (2019). Women in powerful conversation: Collaborative autoethnography and academia. *International Journal of Qualitative Studies in Education, 33*(4), 393–403.

Anderson, V., Rabello, R., Wass, R., Golding, C., Rangi, A., Eteuati, E., …, & Waller, A. (2020). Good teaching as care in higher education. *Higher Education, 79*(1), 1–19.

Arvaja, M. (2024). Constructing teacher self in a dialogue between multiple I-positions: A case from teacher education. *Journal of Constructivist Psychology, 37*(4), 451–471.

Bakhtin, M. M. (1994). *The Bakhtin reader.* Edward Arnold.

Becher, T., & Trowler, P. (2001). *Academic tribes and territories.* McGraw-Hill Education.

Biggs, J., Hawley, P. H., & Biernat, M. (2018). The academic conference as a chilly climate for women: Effects of gender representation on experiences of sexism, coping responses, and career intentions. *Sex Roles: A Journal of Research, 78*(5–6), 394–408. https://doi.org/10.1007/s11199-017-0800-9

Blackman, L. (2012). *Immaterial bodies: Affect, embodiment, mediation.* SAGE Publications.

Bochner, A. P., & Ellis, C. (2022). Why autoethnography? *Social Work and Social Sciences Review, 23*(2), 8–18.

Brooks, S. D., Dean, A. S., Franklin-Phipps, A., Mathis, E., Rath, C. L., Raza, N., …, & Sundstrom, K. (2020). Becoming-academic in the neoliberal academy: A collective biography. *Gender and Education, 32*(3), 281–300.

Canagarajah, A. S. (2012). Teacher development in a global profession: An autoethnography. *TESOL Quarterly, 46*(2), 258–279. https://doi.org/10.1002/tesq.18

Case, K. (2017). Insider without: Journey across the working-class academic arc. *Journal of Working-Class Studies, 2*(2), 16–35.

Cruz, C. (2021). The melancholia of class: A manifesto for the working class. *Repeater Books.*

De Luca Picione, R. (2021). The dynamic nature of the human psyche and its three tenets: Normativity, liminality, and resistance—Semiotic advances in direction of modal articulation sensemaking. *Human Arenas, 4*(2), 279–293.

Deardorff, D. K. (2006). Identification and assessment of intercultural competence as a student outcome of internationalization. *Journal of Studies in International Education, 10*(3), 241–266. https://doi.org/10.1177/1028315306287002
Fanon, F. (1967). *Black skin, white masks* (C. L. Markmann, Trans.). Grove Press. (Original work published 1952).
Fiore, T. (1951). *Formiche di Puglia.* Laterza.
Folabit, N. L., & Jita, L. C. (2024). Academics' professional identity: Conflicting personal values of academics and institutional culture. *Interdisciplinary Journal of Sociality Studies, 4*, 1–13. https://doi.org/10.38140/ijss-2024.vol4.05
Fossa, P. (Ed.). (2022). *New perspectives on inner speech* (pp. 65–80). Springer.
Friedman, S. (2016). Habitus clivé and the emotional imprint of social mobility. *The Sociological Review, 64*(1), 129–147.
Furness, Z. (Ed.). (2012). *Punkademics: The basement show in the Ivory Tower.* Minor Compositions.
Gaulejac, V. (2016). *La névrose de classe* (Nouvelle édition actualisée). Éditions Payot & Rivages.
Gill, R. (2014). Academics, cultural workers and critical labour studies. *Journal of Cultural Economy, 7*(1), 12–30. https://doi.org/10.1080/17530350.2013.861763
Giroux, H. A. (1993). Living dangerously: Identity politics and the new cultural racism: Towards a critical pedagogy of representation. *Cultural Studies, 7*(1), 1–27. https://doi.org/10.1080/09502389300490021
Grossen, M., & Muller Mirza, N. (2020). Talking about cultural diversity at school: Dialogical tensions and obstacles to secondarisation. *European Journal of Psychology of Education, 35*(2), 243–264.
Henderson, E. F., & Moreau, M. P. (2019). Carefree conferences? Academics with caring responsibilities performing mobile academic subjectivities. *Gender and Education, 32*(1), 70–85. https://doi.org/10.1080/09540253.2019.1685654
Hermans, H. J. M. (2013). The dialogical self in education: Introduction. *Journal of Constructivist Psychology, 26*(2), 81–89. https://doi.org/10.1080/10720537.2013.759018
Hermans, H. J. M., & Gieser, T. (Eds.). (2011). *Handbook of dialogical self theory.* Cambridge University Press.
Hermans, H. J. M., & Hermans-Konopka, A. (2010). *Dialogical self theory: Positioning and counter-positioning in a globalizing society.* Cambridge University Press.
Humphreys, M., & Brown, A. D. (2017). Narratives of organizational identity and identification: A case study of hegemony and resistance. In S. Minahan (Ed.), *The aesthetic turn in management* (pp. 279–305). Routledge.
Impedovo, M. A. (2022). Transformative agency in workers' account: Tensions in professional development. *Migration Letters, 19*(3), 343–355.
Impedovo, M. A., & Ferreira-Meyers, K. (2021). Authority, collective learning and agentic action in teaching: Tracing a pedagogy from Franz Fanon. *Education in the North, 28*(1), 135–152. https://doi.org/10.26203/agdv-0563
Impedovo, M., & Ligorio, M. B. (2025). Teacher practices observation enriched by collective discussion: Teacher noticing as I-position. *Journal of Constructivist Psychology*, 1–24.
Konopka, A., Hermans, H. J., & Gonçalves, M. M. (2018). The dialogical self as a landscape of mind populated by a society of I-positions. In *Handbook of dialogical self theory and psychotherapy* (pp. 9–23). Routledge.

Lee, E. M. (2017). Where people like me don't belong: Faculty members from low-socioeconomic-status backgrounds. *Sociology of Education, 90*(3), 197–212. https://doi.org/10.1177/0038040717710495

Lendák-Kabók, K. (2020). Women's work–life balance strategies in academia. *Journal of Family Studies, 28*(3), 1139–1157. https://doi.org/10.1080/13229400.2020.1802324

Marginson, S., & Rhoades, G. (2002). Beyond national states, markets, and systems of higher education: A glonacal agency heuristic. *Higher Education, 43*(3), 281–309. https://doi.org/10.1023/A:1014699605875

Markides, J., Cross, B., & Chowdhury, S. A. (2021). *Wayfinding conversations: Rethinking education to disrupt marginality.* Education in the North.

Monereo, C., & Hermans, H. (2023). Education and dialogical self: State of art (Educación y yo dialógico: Estado de la cuestión). *Journal for the Study of Education and Development, 46*(3), 445–491.

Roberts, A. (2024). The polycrisis of capitalism. *Theory & Struggle, 125*(1), 40–55.

Schratz, M., Schwarz, J. F., & Westfall-Greiter, T. (2013). Looking at two sides of the same coin: Phenomenologically oriented vignette research and its implications for teaching and learning. *Studia paedagogica, 18*(4), 57–73.

Stenberg, K., & Maaranen, K. (2020). The differences between beginning and advanced student teachers' teacher identities based on their practical theories. *Education Inquiry, 11*(3), 196–210.

Timperley, C., Sutherland, K. A., Wilson, M., & Hall, M. (2020). He moana pukepuke: Navigating gender and ethnic inequality in early career academics' conference attendance. *Gender and Education, 32*(1), 11–26. https://doi.org/10.1080/09540253.2019.1633464

Uriko, K. (2019). Dialogical self and the changing body during the transition to motherhood. *Journal of Constructivist Psychology, 32*(3), 221–235.

Valsiner, J. (2014). *An invitation to cultural psychology.* Sage.

von Fircks, E. F. (2024). The dialogical self of Taoistic dynamics: How scientists and practitioners can trigger the discovery of a harmonious self. *Integrative Psychological and Behavioral Science, 58*(2), 361–385.

Warnock, D. M. (2016). Paradise lost? Patterns and precarity in working-class academic narratives. *Journal of Working-Class Studies, 1*(1), 28–44.

Weick, K. E., & Weick, K. E. (1995). *Sensemaking in organizations* (Vol. *3,* pp. 10–1002). Sage publications.

Wortham, S. E. F. (2001). *Narratives in action: A strategy for research and analysis.* Teachers College Press.

Zembylas, M., & Papamichael, E. (2017). Pedagogies of discomfort and empathy in multicultural teacher education. *Intercultural Education, 28*(1), 1–19. https://doi.org/10.1080/14675986.2017.1288448

CHAPTER 2

TEACHER NOTICING AS SELF-PORTRAITURE: RELATIONAL PRACTICES

ABSTRACT

Teachers and academics increasingly experience emotional stress, often feeling overwhelmed, undervalued, and disconnected from their work, because of heightened performance demands and accountability pressures. The chapter questions how to shape inner professional life with the process of noticing, contributing in a regenerative way to their daily experience of teaching. Specifically, the chapter explores the role of teacher noticing as a dialogical, relational, and identity-forming process, drawing on Dialogical Self Theory as a central theoretical lens. Through art-based analogy, based on Rembrandt's practice of self-portraiture as self-inquiry, and vignette, collected in the last academic year from my experience as a teacher educator, I conceptualise noticing as an affective, ethical, and reflexive engagement with one's multiple identity positions. Teacher noticing results as a dialogical practice embedded in the affective life.

Keywords: Teachers; emotional stress; noticing; reflexivity; identity formation

INTRODUCTION

The commodification of education, academic labour, and the contested emphasis on 'impact' and quantifiable outputs have become normalised features of the higher education landscape in the neoliberal era

---

Teacher Dialogical Self, pages 25–37

doi:10.1108/978-1-80686-957-220261003

(Ling & Livingston, 2023; Sutton, 2017). Research has shown that teachers and academics increasingly experience emotional stress, often feeling overwhelmed, undervalued, and disconnected from their work, because of heightened performance demands and accountability pressures (Fecho et al., 2016; Maisuria & Helmes, 2019; Uptin et al., 2016). This strain can possibly lead to stress, burnout, passivity (Janfada et al., 2025) and, ultimately, alienation. Alienation is a multifaceted concept, often loosely used to describe the process through which individuals become estranged from themselves and from their social relationships (Hascher & Hadjar, 2018; Morinaj & Hascher, 2019) – saturated also with social media and online influencers (Çetinkaya, 2025; Wani et al., 2024). While alienation is often seen as a deficit, it can also be reinterpreted as a potential precursor to emancipation – a state that creates the conditions for critical awareness and transformative action (Tau et al., 2024). Indeed, the growing vulnerabilities in contemporary society (Marcadal, 2021; Nixon & Scullion, 2022) underscore the need for regeneration in education, both for teachers and for students.

In line with this perspective, the chapter argues that personal action and the affective experiences of both educators and students constitute powerful strategies for confronting the uncertainties of academic life (Giroux, 2014; Zembylas, 2021).

Specifically, we explore a micro-act inside the daily activity of the teaching: the practice of 'noticing'. Far from being a passive internal state, noticing functions as an active competence – an embodied awareness that bridges impression and expression. However, relatively little research has examined the link between noticing and teachers' knowledge (Schoenfeld, 2011), and even fewer studies have considered its connection to affect and emotions (for one example of case study, see Impedovo & Ligorio, 2025).

The chapter is structured as follows. First, I articulate the theoretical conceptualisation of the dialogical nature of teacher identity in relation to the act of noticing. I then examine two vignettes (Schratz et al., 2013) drawn from everyday practices as a teacher-educator. The first vignette illustrates a brief moment of attentional shift – from the external to the internal and back again – set in parallel with Rembrandt's practice of self-portraiture as a form of self-inquiry. The second vignette highlights the relational dimension inherent in the act of noticing. The third vignette focuses on the interplay between internal and interpersonal side in the act of noticing, tracing three levels of noticing.

In the final discussion, I conceptualise noticing as an affective and reflexive engagement with one's multiple identity positions. Ultimately, teacher noticing emerges as a dialogical practice deeply embedded in affective life.

TEACHER NOTICING

Teachers could potentially act as an observer of each given moment composing classroom life. However, teachers cannot observe everything given the 'blooming, buzzing confusion of sensory data' that are abundant in classrooms (Sherin & Star, 2011, p. 69). And, more or less spontaneously, they have to select what to focus on and how to interpret their observations to adapt their activity according to students' learning. This attentional work of observation is referred to as teacher noticing (Sherin & Star, 2011). Teacher noticing has become lately a prominent construct in research on teacher education and professional development (for a review, Chan et al., 2021; König et al., 2022).

It is understood as two interconnected processes: how teachers selectively observe classroom events and how they interpret these observations (Sherin & van Es, 2009; van Es & Sherin, 2021). This noticing makes the teachers at the same time active and constrained in directing and focussing their attention on certain aspects, while potentially overlooking others (Erickson, 2011, p. 17). For instance, if teachers focus on pedagogy or classroom management, which is what they do most frequently (Wolff et al., 2016), they may not simultaneously notice students' thinking. Recognising students' thinking is crucial for making responsive, real-time decisions (Richards et al., 2020). In this way, teachers can be highly effective in adjusting their lessons based on their insights about their students (Schoenfeld, 2011). Nevertheless, noticing students' thinking is not always standard practice, and simply having teaching experience does not ensure that teachers will develop this skill (Jacobs et al., 2010).

While research has explored the benefits of different methods for noticing students' thinking, particularly in mathematics (Erickson, 2011) or during school intervention (Rainio & Hofmann, 2021), studies emphasise the positive impact of learning to notice in the context of teacher education (Erickson, 2011).

THEORETICAL FRAMEWORK: DIALOGICAL SELF THEORY AND TEACHER NOTICING

The theoretical framework is grounded in Dialogical Self Theory (DST), which conceptualises the self as a dynamic multiplicity of 'I-positions' – autonomous perspectives or voices that coexist within an internal dialogical space. These positions are shaped by personal experience, social interactions, cultural norms, institutional structures, and historical context. Within this internal dialogical space, these voices continuously engage, negotiate, and reconfigure the self in response to changing contexts.

DST emphasises that internal dialogs are not merely solitary reflections; they are deeply interwoven with the voices of others – real or imagined. As Hermans and Gieser (2011) note, the self is situated in time and space yet remains capable of shifting between positions as circumstances evolve. This constant negotiation, both internally and externally, gives rise to professional identity, which Grossen and Muller Mirza (2020) describe as emerging through interaction and relationship.

Importantly, 'the other' in DST goes beyond direct interpersonal encounters. It includes the internalized presence of others – institutions, traditions, colleagues, family, and friends – that shape the dialogical process (Marková, 2003). These voices mediate the self's understanding and position-taking, forming a spectrum of I-positions that reflect both personal identity and the perspectives of significant others (Henry & Mollstedt, 2021a; 2021b).

In educational contexts, DST offers a compelling lens for examining the noticing practices of teachers – the ways they attend to and interpret students' behaviour, classroom dynamics, and their own instructional actions (Mason, 2002). This perspective highlights the fluidity with which teachers shift positions – such as between authority and empathy, or between established practices and emergent responses – within their professional role.

This internal negotiation fosters a professional identity that is adaptive yet coherent, shaped through continual dialogical engagement. Fecho's (2011) concept of 'wobble' offers valuable insight into teacher development. Wobble refers to moments of uncertainty, tension, or instability in practice that prompt reflective questioning and potential growth. Rather than viewing these moments as setbacks, Fecho frames them as openings for deeper understanding. Through recursive internal dialogs, teachers confront dilemmas, recalibrate their beliefs, and refine their pedagogical choices. In the following sections, the dialogical nature of identity is explored in relation to the act of noticing through the analysis of three vignettes drawn from everyday practices as teacher-educators.

INNER NOTICING: TEACHING AS SELF-PORTRAITURE

In the following, I use a vignette – collected in the last academic year from my experience as a teacher educator – to bring one example of application of the noticing act in the classroom.

> *I am looking around for a few seconds.*
>
> *My gaze drifts outward, where sunlight meets the leaves swaying in the wind. I follow the movement of the leaves while simultaneously feeling my breath slow down. The students are engaged, so I can maintain low vigilance. A few other outside sounds catch my attention, but I don't dwell on them.*
>
> *I bring my gaze back to the students, to the many colourful objects that surround each of them. The colours are vibrant – I take this note of liveliness with me. I pause to observe the class for a few seconds, without focussing on anyone or anything.*
>
> *My gaze absorbs. The situation becomes interesting, more engaging than my thoughts about the follow-up of the lesson. My emotional state shifts: I feel calmer and once again open to interaction, discussion, exchange with the students. I'm ready to engage again.*

This moment of attentional shift, from the external to the internal and back again, marks more than a sensory observation – it becomes an act of inner noticing. In the classroom, such moments are often fleeting, yet they reveal the deeper dimensions of teacher awareness: of students, of the learning environment, and crucially, of the self in relation to both.

In this context, the concept of teacher noticing (Chan et al., 2021; Sherin & Star, 2011) gains resonance. Teachers continuously filter the richness of the classroom through their gaze, deciding what to attend to, what to interpret, and how to act in ways that respond to students' learning. This noticing is not simply a technical skill but a cognitive-emotional capacity that is simultaneously active and limited (Erickson, 2011). While teachers often notice pedagogical routines or classroom management concerns (Wolff et al., 2016), deeper noticing – particularly of students' thinking – requires purposeful cultivation (Jacobs et al., 2010; Richards et al., 2020). It is not automatically acquired with experience, nor is it neutral; it is shaped by the values, assumptions, and emotional states that the teacher brings into the classroom. To understand the full depth of teacher noticing, we might look to Rembrandt's practice of self-portraiture as an analogous form of inquiry. Across his lifetime, Rembrandt painted himself over 80 times – not out of vanity, but as a method of self-examination (see Fig. 3). His portraits do not merely depict physical likeness but express evolving emotional states, vulnerabilities, and reflections on ageing, failure, and identity. In this way, each brushstroke becomes a tool for noticing the self-seeing, for attending to one's own presence and transformation in the time. Like Rembrandt, the teacher could become attentive to inner and external change, claim more sensibility to the repetitive and (im)previsible teaching situations in the classroom. Such a parallel helps us frame reflexive noticing as a practice akin to Rembrandt's painterly introspection.

Reflexive noticing extends beyond mere recognition of classroom events. It asks teachers to become aware of the frameworks that shape what they see, to question what remains unseen, and to prepare

Fig. 3. Self-Portrait by Rembrandt 1630 – Unknown Source, Public Domain, https://commons.wikimedia.org/w/index.php?curid=9534124.

themselves emotionally and ethically for what their gaze may uncover. By integrating emotions, identity, and reflexive noticing into pedagogy, educators cultivate inclusive and transformative learning environments (Impedovo, 2025).

Questioning the teaching routines: Where do I look?

This question invites us to consider not just the object of attention, but the position of the self within that act. The teachers navigate around:

- Being: noticing one's own state, emotions, and biases - relationality to self.
- Thinking: the cognitive framing of classroom events - what is assumed, what is questioned.
- Relating: seeing the student not as a role but as a person with their own agency and struggle.
- Collaborating: sharing perspective through dialogic engagement and collective reflection.
- Acting: using noticing not as an endpoint but as a lever for change -for enabling more humane, responsive education.

In this light, noticing becomes a micro-act of emancipation from the repetition of the teaching routines and renovation of attention. Like the painter choosing to confront their reflection on canvas, the teacher's gaze can become a way to reclaim subjectivity within institutional structures that often flatten it. In an era marked by metrics, commodification, and alienation (Nixon & Scullion, 2022; Sutton, 2017), this type of awareness affirms the affective, relational, and ethical dimensions of teaching. To notice is not only to see, but to care, to feel, to understand, and ultimately, to act (De Kadt & Jawitz, 2018). Like Rembrandt's self-portraits, it invites us to see the cracks, the contradictions, the humanity – and in doing so, to remain open to the ongoing reformation of both teacher and student.

NOTICING AS RELATIONAL PRACTICE

In the following, I use a second vignette to stress the relational dimension involved in the act of noticing.

> *Yesterday morning, I experienced a subtle but significant shift: instead of reacting defensively to the critical tone of some colleagues who were judging others' work in the school office, I chose to listen.*
>
> *I listened not to agree, but to understand. I let it be rooted in receptivity rather than judgement, in attentiveness rather than resistance.*
>
> *And in doing so, I gained clarity, not only about the situation but also about a small opportunity – an opening to access information that might benefit not only myself but also other teachers, in a setting where conflict often blocks communication.*

Through gentle acceptance of others even when I did not approve of their stance, I noticed something essential: how often we lose the possibility to shift the course of events when we let our reactive selves lead. And how much negativity we unknowingly nourish when we close ourselves off.

This moment is not merely an anecdote, but an entry into the practice of relational noticing – a way of attending that is both inwardly and outwardly oriented. It invites a type of presence where care, discernment, and judgement are not separate faculties, but intertwined capacities. This echoes what Scharmer (2007) calls *presencing* – a state of embodied attention in which perception is guided not just by cognition but also by care. It can be describes as a mode of sensing that is ethically and affectively grounded.

Noticing, in this frame, is not static; it is dynamic, co-constitutive, and dialogical. It operates through loops – between outer perception and inner response, between embodied awareness and social meaning-making.

From this perspective, the classroom, the corridor, and the staff meeting – all become relational fields where noticing becomes a form of world-making. As teachers, our attentional acts are not neutral. What we choose to see, or fail to see, what we choose to interpret or ignore, actively shapes the relational climate around us. Our care, concern, and even discomfort is transacted into pedagogical action. To manage this transition, it requires what Rainio and Hofmann (2021) call reflexive noticing – a recursive process of preparing to notice, noticing, and reflecting on what has been noticed. Through repeated cycles, an inner space opens where trust, curiosity, and ethical responsiveness can emerge. Such space fosters not only pedagogical responsiveness but also a deeper, relational agency – one grounded in openness to the present and to the other.

In this light, noticing is not only a professional skill, but also a relational ethic. It involves:

- Being-with-self: noticing one's internal states, impulses, and judgements with awareness.
- Being with others: recognising the affective atmosphere of encounters and choosing care over reaction.
- Being-in-the-larger context: perceiving situations as part of broader ecological and institutional realities, while remaining open to change.

By practicing this kind of noticing, we participate in shaping more educational spaces where attentiveness becomes an act of resistance against disconnection, and a seed for transformation.

THREE LEVELS OF TEACHING NOTICING

The third vignette focuses on the interplay between internal and interpersonal side in the act of noticing.

> *This morning, I had a meaningful conversation with a student. As I listened attentively to her questions, I tried to hold not only her perspective but also the broader framework of our shared learning context.*
>
> *This effort allowed me to step outside of my usual way of thinking and resist responding from a fixed position.*
>
> *Instead of offering a definitive answer, I invited her to explore the issue through some questions, encouraging a shared process of inquiry.*

What emerged was an unexpected realization: if I genuinely want to work on myself as an educator, I cannot hold rigidly to my personal opinions. To move towards a deeper truth, I am willing to welcome opposing perspectives. In doing so, I felt a part of my habitual attachment to 'being right' dissolve. What remained was a sense of light shift towards openness that I want to remember and cultivate. This moment illustrates the practice of relational noticing – a way of seeing that is not limited to what we observe, but how we position ourselves in relation to what we see. It echoes the model proposed by a recent work (Impedovo & Ligorio, 2025), who articulate three dynamic 'I-positions' of teacher noticing:

1. I-as-Observer: at this foundational level, the teacher observes students primarily from an external stance – focussing on behaviours, engagement, and understanding. The aim is to gather data that can inform instructional planning. It is often the first step in developing awareness of students' needs and classroom dynamics.
2. I-as-Teacher with Students' Observer. In this second position, the teacher's lens broadens to include their own actions and decisions. It involves recognising how teaching strategies, relational stances, and instructional choices impact students' learning. This level demands a more complex dual awareness: of students and of self-in-practice.
3. Meta-Position as Observer of the Context. The third level introduces a systemic lens. Teachers begin to view themselves as embedded in a wider ecology – shaped by institutional norms, cultural narratives, physical environments, and unseen power dynamics. This level aligns with what Teo and Febbraro (2024) call autoepistemic reflexivity – a form of self-inquiry that interrogates not only what is known, but also how it is known, and what remains ignored. It requires stepping back to question assumptions and to reflect on the interdependence of people, structures, and histories. This level invites us to expand reflective gaze beyond individual practice to the broader systems in which teaching and learning take place. It also underscores the need for collaborative dialogue with peers and diverse perspectives to enrich individual insight and support sustained professional growth (Monereo, 2022).

By moving intentionally through these levels of engagement, teachers develop a more holistic capacity to see students not only as learners but as co-constructors of meaning within a dynamic and interrelated environment (Impedovo & Ligorio, 2025). In doing so, they cultivate not only professional efficacy but also ethical responsibility in shaping inclusive and resonant learning spaces (Hyde, 2024).

Noticing for a Vibrant Pedagogy

Noticing, in the context of education, goes beyond the cognitive act of perceiving – it becomes an act of well-being. At its core lies what Scharmer (2007) calls the power of we – a collective capacity to transform schools into spaces where learners generate actions and insights from within themselves. This understanding calls for an expanded view on that resonates with both inner and outer worlds. Such resonance reflects contemporary interdisciplinary perspectives that consider how individual affective responses are not innate, but culturally and contextually constructed (Barrett, 2017). This interplay between inner experience and external reality positions noticing as a relational and situated practice (Impedovo, 2026). This process begins with attentiveness, learners and teachers alike are seized – grasped by an experience that opens them to new ways of being. This act requires biographical reflection – asking: (Jaakkola et al., 2022): *Where do I come from? How are my values and assumptions shaped? What do I stand for?*

With this foundation of self-knowledge and meta – reflective questions, the teachers underpin transformative pedagogical action, essential to leading systemic change.

CONCLUSION

The chapter argues how noticing becomes inherently relational, not only in terms of how teachers perceive and respond to students, but also in how they respond to themselves as pedagogical agents-in-motion. As teachers notice students' behaviour, emotions, and learning processes, they simultaneously notice their own reactions, assumptions, and internal shifts. This recursive loop of noticing fosters reflexivity, where internal dialogue serves as the bridge between professional action and personal meaning-making. It is in these reflective moments – what Fecho (2011) calls 'wobbles' – that the self-encounters the unfamiliar within the familiar, allowing for growth through inner tension. This noticing process is dialogical in nature (Marková, 2006): the voices of colleagues, cultural narratives, institutional expectations, and students' feedback all echo in the teacher's internal space. Thus, noticing is an ethical and relational practice, where the educator assumes responsibility not only for the act of perceiving but for the relational consequences of how they choose to respond, both to others and to themselves. Through this lens, teaching is an act of relational authorship, a constantly revised self-portrait informed by the dialogical negotiation of identity within the pedagogical encounter.

REFERENCES

Barrett, L. F. (2017). The theory of constructed emotion: An active inference account of interoception and categorization. *Social Cognitive and Affective Neuroscience, 12*(1), 1–23.

Çetinkaya, C. (2025). *The politics of misinformation: Social media, polarization, and the geopolitical landscape in 2025: Trend report 6.* https://www.oiip.ac.at/en/publications/

the-politics-of-misinformation-social-media-polarization-and-the-geopolitical-landscape-in-2025/3

Chan, K. K. H., Xu, L., Cooper, R., Berry, A., & van Driel, J. H. (2021). Teacher noticing in science education: Do you see what I see? *Studies in Science Education, 57*(1), 1–44.

De Kadt, E., & Jawitz, J. (2018). Exploring discomfort and care in the experience of a national academic staff development programme. *Critical Studies in Teaching and Learning, 6*(2).

Erickson, F. (2011). On noticing teacher noticing. In M. G. Sherin, V. R. Jacobs, & R. A. Philipp (Eds.), *Mathematics teacher noticing: Seeing through teachers' eyes* (pp. 17–34). Routledge.

Fecho, B., Falter, M., & Hong, X. (2016). *Teaching outside the box but inside the standards: Making room for dialogue.* Teachers College Press.

Fecho, B. (2011). *Teaching for the students: Habits of heart, mind, and practice in the engaged classroom.* Teachers College Press.

Giroux, H. (2014). *Neoliberalism's war on higher education.* Haymarket Books.

Grossen, M., & Muller Mirza, N. (2020). Talking about cultural diversity at school: Dialogical tensions and obstacles to secondarisation. *European Journal of Psychology of Education, 35*(2), 243–264. https://doi.org/10.1007/s10212-019-00442-8

Hascher, T., & Hadjar, A. (2018). School alienation: Theoretical approaches and educational research. *Educational Research, 60*(2), 171–188. https://doi.org/10.1080/00131881.2018.1443021

Henry, A., & Mollstedt, M. (2021a). The other in the self: Mentoring relationships and adaptive dynamics in preservice teacher identity construction. *Learning, Culture and Social Interaction, 31,* 100568. https://doi.org/10.1016/j.lcsi.2021.100568

Henry, M., & Mollstedt, M. (2021b). Dialogical approaches in education: Understanding internal I-positions and the noticing process. *Journal of Educational Research, 45*(3), 120–134.

Hermans, H. J. M., & Gieser, T. (Eds.) (2011). *Handbook of dialogical self theory.* University Press.

Hyde, B. (2024). Teacher reflection as a research method: Using phenomenology to reflect on classroom events. *International Journal of Research and Method in Education.* https://doi.org/10.1080/1743727X.2024.2336142

Impedovo, M. (2026). Affective noticing as a pedagogical tool. In A. Dania & M. Impedovo (Eds.), *Affectivity as pedagogy in the classroom interdisciplinary approaches to relationship-based practice in education.* Routledge.

Impedovo, M., & Ligorio, M. B. (2025). Teacher practices observation enriched by collective discussion: Teacher noticing as I-position. *Journal of Constructivist Psychology,* 1–24.

Impedovo, M. (2025). Socio-cultural analysis: Reflexive noticing as conditions for acting inclusive pedagogy. *Pedagogia delle differenze, 1,* 113–130. https://www.pedagogiadelledifferenze.it

Jaakkola, N., Karvinen, M., Hakio, K., Wolff, L. A., Mattelmäki, T., & Friman, M. (2022, May). Becoming self-aware—How do self-awareness and transformative learning fit in the sustainability competency discourse? *Frontiers in Education, 7,* 855583.

Jacobs, V. R., Lamb, L. L., & Philipp, R. A. (2010). Professional noticing of children's mathematical thinking. *Journal for Research in Mathematics Education, 41*(2), 169–202.

Janfada, M., Lin, A. M., Lim, F. V., & Liu, J. E. (2025). Emotional (dis/un) entanglement in becoming an academic in the neoliberal era: Dialogising transnational accounts of being, thinking and feeling. *International Journal of Applied Linguistics, 35*, 3. https://doi.org/10.1111/ijal.12724

König, J., Santagata, R., Scheiner, T., Adleff, A. K., Yang, X., & Kaiser, G. (2022). Teacher noticing: A systematic literature review of conceptualizations, research designs, and findings on learning to notice. *Educational Research Review, 36*, 100453. https://doi.org/10.1016/j.edurev.2022.100453

Ling, L., & Livingston, K. (2023). *Universities in times of crisis and disruption: Dislocated complexity*. Taylor & Francis.

Maisuria, A., & Helmes, S. (2019). *Life for the academic in the neoliberal university* (1st ed.). Routledge. https://doi.org/10.4324/9780429329951

Marcadal, T. M. (2021). *Social vulnerability*. EBSCO Research Starters. https://www.ebsco.com/research-starters/psychology/social-vulnerability

Marková, I. (2006). On the "Inner Alter" in dialogue. *International Journal for Dialogical Science, 1*(1), 125–147.

Mason, J. (2002). *Researching your own practice: The discipline of noticing*. Routledge.

Monereo, C. (2022). Aprender de las crisis. Los incidentes críticos como metodología para educar, también, emocionalmente. *Revista Internacional de Educación Emocional y Bienestar, 3*(1), 18–19. https://doi.org/10.48102/rieeb.2023.3.1.43

Morinaj, J., & Hascher, T. (2019). School alienation and student well-being: A cross-lagged longitudinal analysis. *European Journal of Psychology of Education, 34*(2), 273–294. https://doi.org/10.1007/s10212-018-0381-1

Nixon, E., & Scullion, R. (2022). Academic labour as professional service work? A psychosocial analysis of emotion in lecturer–student relations under marketization. *Human Relations, 75*(9), 1798–1823.

Rainio, A. P., & Hofmann, R. (2021). Teacher professional dialogues during a school intervention: From stabilization to possibility discourse through reflexive noticing. *The Journal of the Learning Sciences, 30*(4–5), 707–746.

Richards, J., Elby, A., Luna, M. J., Robertson, A. D., Levin, D. M., & Nyeggen, C. G. (2020). Reframing the responsiveness challenge: A framing-anchored explanatory framework to account for irregularity in novice teachers' attention and responsiveness to student thinking. *Cognition and Instruction, 38*(2), 116–152.

Scharmer, C. O. (2007). *Theory U: Leading from the future as it emerges: The social technology of presencing*. Society for Organizational Learning.

Schoenfeld, A. H. (2011). Noticing matters. A lot. Now what? In M. G. Sherin, V. R. Jacobs, & R. A. Philipp (Eds.), *Mathematics teacher noticing: Seeing through teachers' eyes* (pp. 223–238). Routledge.

Schratz, M., Schwarz, J. F., & Westfall-Greiter, T. (2013). Looking at two sides of the same coin: Phenomenologically oriented vignette research and its implications for teaching and learning. *Studia paedagogica, 18*(4), 57–73.

Sherin, B., & Star, J. R. (2011). Reflections on the study of teacher noticing. In M. G. Sherin, V. R. Jacobs, & R. A. Philipp (Eds.), *Mathematics teacher noticing: Seeing through teachers' eyes* (pp. 66–78). Routledge.

Sherin, M. G., & van Es, E. A. (2009). Effects of video club participation on teachers' professional vision. *Journal of Teacher Education, 60*(1), 20–37.

Sutton, P. (2017). Lost souls? The demoralization of academic labour in the measured university. *Higher Education Research and Development, 36*(3), 625–636.

Tau, R., Kloetzer, L., Sacher, A., Zolotareva, A., & Abebayehu, Y. (2024). Alienation and emancipation at the university through performing arts. *Scenario: A Journal of Performative Teaching, Learning, Research,* 16–36.

Teo, T., & Febbraro, A. R. (2024). Modeling and theorizing in psychology: Autoepistemology and epistemic EDI (equity, diversity, and inclusion) as tools for challenging racism. *Review of General Psychology.* https://doi.org/10.1177/10892680241261053

Uptin, J., Barnes, N., Hartung, C., McMahon, S., O'Flynn, G., & Welch, R. (2016). Beyond the academic precariat: A collective biography of poetic subjectivities in the neoliberal university. *Sport, Education and Society, 22*(1), 40–57. https://doi.org/10.1080/13573322.2016.1202227

van Es, E. A., & Sherin, M. G. (2021). Expanding on prior conceptualizations of teacher noticing. *ZDM – Mathematics Education, 53*(1), 17–27. https://doi.org/10.1007/s11858-020-01211-4

Wani, Z. A., Bhat, A., Vishnoi, V., Praveen, H., Simon, N. H., & Hephzibah, D. (2024). Impact of social media on society: A literature review. *Asian Journal of Education and Social Studies, 50*(4), 320–328.

Wolff, C. E., Jarodzka, H., van den Bogert, N., & Boshuizen, H. P. (2016). Teacher vision: Expert and novice teachers' perception of problematic classroom management scenes. *Instructional Science, 44,* 243–265.

Zembylas, M. (2021). The affective dimension of everyday resistance: Implications for critical pedagogy in engaging with neoliberalism's educational impact. *Critical Studies in Education, 62*(2), 211–226.

CHAPTER 3

THE LIVED EXPERIENCE AS A PROFESSIONAL POSSIBILITY

ABSTRACT

Drawing on qualitative teacher narrative accounts and journaling as a self-explorative technique, this chapter examines how everyday interactions – including materiality like with textbooks, lesson preparations, and classroom resources – constitute events through which teachers co-construct meaning related to their professional development. The chapter highlights how including attention to materiality fosters professional events that are responsive, relational, and open to emergent possibilities. Implications for pedagogies are discussed.

Keywords: Everyday interactions; teacher; pedagogy; event; lived experience; affect theory

INTRODUCTION

In this chapter we focus on the relational moments in which professional development actually takes shape. Yet, what truly marks a turning point in a teacher's growth is not always content or technique, but the lived event – a moment of rupture or intensity that reorganises understanding and expands one's relation to practice. The event carries value not because of its external structure, but due to its inner intensity, its affective and reflective weight. It becomes a site of meaning-making, transformation, and reorientation.

Teacher Dialogical Self, pages 39–46

doi:10.1108/978-1-80686-957-220261004

Following Roth's (2024) suggestion, if we treat the event as the minimal unit of analysis, we reposition our lens from static categories towards dynamic, situated encounters that hold the potential to reconfigure how teachers think, feel, and act. The event is not reducible to a discrete 'happening' in chronological time. Rather, it is an emergent configuration of relations – a constellation in which people, bodies, materials, discourses, and emotions intersect in ways that cannot be fully anticipated. It is often marked by a certain force – a rupture, interruption, or intensification that unsettles existing patterns and invites reorientation.

From this standpoint, the micro becomes not a reduction of complexity but a necessary entry point for apprehending the processual nature of professional becoming. Small shifts – a hesitation before responding to a student, the subtle rephrasing of a question, a sudden recognition in a colleague's gaze – can catalyse transformations in a teacher's professional identity and pedagogical sensibilities.

In everyday life, many actions are repeated regularly – acts performed under the influence of routine. Yet, there is a difference between acting out of habit and experiencing an action with curiosity. One creativity of the teacher is expressed in activating reflective attention and allowing new meanings to emerge through the resonance of memory, emotion, and situated perception.

When the event is foregrounded, the temporality of teacher learning shifts from long-term 'developmental stages' to moments of potential embedded in everyday practice. Professional growth is not seen solely as a linear accumulation of skills but as a series of situated intensities, each carrying the possibility of new orientations.

By holding the event as the analytical unit, teacher educators can better capture the situated, relational, and affective texture of professional learning – elements that are often flattened when data is aggregated into categories or themes detached from their moment of occurrence.

The chapter is so structured. First, we first examine socio-material events and the concept of the dialogical self.

To illustrate these ideas, we present two narrative accounts by young teacher-students that highlight key moments of tension and uncertainty in everyday teaching practice – what can be understood as dilemma events (Tan et al., 2015). These moments reveal the complex interplay between the teacher's intentions, student responses, and the material and social conditions of the classroom.

In addition, an illustrative example of journaling (Diseth, 2025; Dreyer, 2015) is employed as a methodology for self-exploration in teachers' professional development.

By reflecting on specific teaching episodes, teachers and teacher educators can examine the internal and external dialogs that shape their practice.

SOCIO-MATERIAL EVENT AND DIALOGICAL SELF

Hubert Hermans conceptualised the Self as polyphonic, consisting of multiple I-positions shaped through the selective internalisation of voices from significant others encountered across one's life (Hermans, 1996). He described their interrelations through the metaphor of a 'society of the Self' (Hermans, 2013). The analytical perspective adopted in this chapter draws primarily on Bakhtin's notion of voice (Bakhtin, 1986). Such voices may belong to individuals physically present in the exchange, to absent interlocutors, or to broader social entities expressed through participants' speech (Grossen & Salazar Orvig, 2011). This has been described as generalised voices (Linell, 2009) or cultural voices (Wegerif, 2013). As Marková et al. (2007) point out, speakers cannot be considered the sole authors of their utterances. Both literary and everyday discourse are interwoven with multiple voices – some explicit, others implicit – that arise from prior dialogs or discourses the speaker has encountered. From a methodological standpoint, the concept of voice offers a valuable lens for identifying and interpreting the plurality of perspectives within dialogic interactions. However, traditional applications of dialogical theory in psychology and education have tended to privilege human voices, neglecting the contribution of the material environment. More recent work has foregrounded the role of materiality in dialogical processes (e.g., Hetherington et al., 2018), particularly in technology-mediated learning (Mehto et al., 2020). Narratives of educational experience thus provide fertile ground for examining how human and non-human agents co-act in shaping learning environments (Latour, 2005). This polyphonic orchestration underscores how social and material agencies are intertwined in educational encounters and invites future inquiry into the ways researchers' own multiple voices participate in constructing the dialogical–material terrain of educational research.

Within teacher professional development, events function as focal points where multiple voices and material affordances intersect, shaping how teachers position themselves and reinterpret their practices. By attending events, researchers can trace how dialogical and material forces are orchestrated in real time, providing a grounded view of how professional learning unfolds in practice. This perspective makes it possible to link the theoretical insights of the dialogical–material approach with the empirical examination of teacher growth, capturing both the polyphonic character of interaction and the embodied, situated nature of professional development.

METHODOLOGY: DILEMMA EVENTS BY YOUNG TEACHER-STUDENTS

Considering that the process of semiosis is affective in its nature (Valsiner, 2024, p. 10), the following narrative accounts illustrate key moments of tension and uncertainty that arise in the everyday practice of young teacher-students (Tan et al., 2015) – what can be described as 'dilemma events'. These are instances where the teacher faces conflicting demands or choices that require reflection, negotiation, and adaptive decision-making. Each account highlights how materiality and dialogue intersect to shape both professional development and student learning. They demonstrate that pedagogical dilemmas are not merely cognitive or procedural challenges, but events in which human and material elements co-constitute the educational experience. Through these examples, we can see how the teacher's decisions, students' responses, and the affordances of classroom materials are entangled, producing emergent forms of meaning and action.

These moments – as proposed in the narrative account of a 23-year-old teacher-student in an elementary school part of a research project - we gain insight into how teaching and learning unfold in dialogical and materially grounded ways.

The Event: Information on Different Resources

This narrative account highlights the tension between the teacher's intentions, the students' needs, and the affordances of materials, emphasising the orchestrating a solution.

The account shows the challenges of navigating different resources, each carrying its own perspective and pedagogical assumptions, and how the teacher negotiates these voices to create coherent lessons.

> *I am thinking about the textbooks I keep at home, most of which are borrowed from the university library. To prepare our lessons, we need – alongside the official documents and official programs – additional pedagogical resources.*
>
> *I use some of these textbooks because they are available in the classroom and shared with my teaching partner. However, I do not own any teacher's editions. I have also had to seek out materials in certain subjects where I had no classroom resources at all (e.g., English, history) or to explore what other publishers offer, since I have not chosen a specific method and am discovering them as I go. My aim is to find alternative didactic approaches that suit me better.*
>
> *Sometimes I take a discovery activity from one textbook and then continue with another, because it seems more accessible and allows me to feel more confident in addressing the topic with my pupils.*
>
> *However, I am aware that this process is very time-consuming, even though I try to limit the number of resources I use. As a result, lesson preparation often takes much longer without necessarily being more effective. In the end, I suspect this may work against me.*
>
> *My mentors have pointed out that, rather than scattering my efforts, it would be better to focus on mastering the methods already in place – at least during this first training year – to follow a clear progression and ensure consistent learning outcomes. Furthermore, these methods are designed to accommodate differentiation, particularly in the context of combined classes.*

The Event: Doing Photocopies

The following second account captures an *event* in which the materiality of classroom resources – the photocopies – interacts with both teacher and pupil. The production and use of these copies mediate the teaching-learning process, revealing students' difficulties with handwriting shape instructional choices. In this event, the teacher negotiates multiple voices while engaging with material artefacts.

> *I am thinking about the issue of the large number of photocopies I am obliged to make. I teach elementary school. My classroom is composed of 25 pupils.*
>
> *I realised that I was producing around 60 copies per working day, between exercises, lesson sheets, and other materials. Yesterday, I printed more than 80 copies. This made me aware that I cannot continue like this. I know that all my pupils experience difficulties with handwriting and copying. If I did not provide printed versions, copying a lesson from the board could take up to 40 minutes – far too long for a single lesson.*
>
> *At the same time, I knew this was not a sustainable solution, both from an environmental perspective and because it does not help pupils improve their skills.*
>
> *If handwriting is so challenging and the task feels so laborious, then we must actually work on it: practice, train, and develop fluency. The difficulty is such that, during copying, they make many mistakes because they struggle to stay focused on the content while dealing with the motor effort itself.*
>
> *I therefore conclude that relying on photocopies to save lesson time is not helping my pupils. I am taking advantage of the fact that I currently work in a school where printing is unrestricted. I must therefore find more sustainable strategies.*

The materials – lesson sheets, paper, writing tools – mediate the students' engagement. At the same time, the teacher's reflection on time management and sustainability reveals a recursive process: her own I-positions as planner, mentor, and reflective practitioner shift in response to these classroom events.

JOURNALING AS A METHODOLOGY FOR SELF-EXPLORATION IN TEACHER PROFESSIONAL DEVELOPMENT

In exploring teacher professional development, journaling offers a powerful methodology for reflective practice and self-exploration (Diseth, 2025; Dreyer, 2015). By maintaining a written or audio record of experiences (Christensen & Weissmann, 2025), dilemmas, and classroom interactions, teachers can trace how these voices interact, conflict, and coalesce over time. Journaling enables teachers to capture both the cognitive and affective dimensions of teaching, revealing how decisions, emotions, and classroom dynamics are entangled with material and social contexts (Kling, & Buhl, 2025). Through journaling, professional experiences become narrative events – moments of reflection in which the teacher observes and interrogates the interplay between their own positions, the students' responses, and the affordances of classroom materials. The practice allows for iterative reconstruction of classroom events, turning routine experiences into opportunities for insight, adaptation, and professional growth. Moreover, journaling provides a structured yet flexible space to explore the materiality of teaching, including how physical resources, classroom organisation, and environmental factors influence pedagogical choices. By self-reflective inquiry, teachers can cultivate a nuanced awareness of the relational and affective forces shaping learning experiences. In this way, journaling becomes both a mirror and a laboratory for professional development – supporting teachers in understanding themselves, their students, and the complex ecosystem of classroom pedagogy.

In the following section, an example of personal journaling.

JOURNALING: CÉZANNE AND MONT SAINTE-VICTOIRE

During the writing process of this chapter, I made a short hiking to Saint Victoir Mont – celebrated by Paul Cézanne painting.[1] Coming back home, I searched online some of the paintings to confront them with my impression from the walk. I found myself wondering what could drive someone to paint around 30 representations of the same subject, Mont Sainte-Victoire. Didn't he ever grow bored of repeating the same motif? As I reflected on this, a parallel question arose for me: how can I, as a teacher, avoid becoming weary of teaching the same material day after day, year after year? Slowly, the answer became clear: affectivity.

I realized that Cézanne's relationship with Mont Sainte-Victoire was not just about seeing a mountain; it was an ongoing dialogue, an affective rapport between himself and his environment. The mountain was not a passive backdrop: each painting became an event that shaped his perception, technique, expression, mood and received an impression by the Mont. I began to see that Cézanne did not simply paint the mountain; he lived with it, interacted with it, and let it become part of his own process of becoming. Each painting became an encounter, carrying forward his engagement with place, time, matter and living bodies - of nature and himself.

This made me think about the idea of a self that is extended into the environment, linked with the rhythms and textures of the world around it. Cézanne's repeated encounters with the mountain reminded me that repetition does not necessarily lead to boredom; instead, it can deepen understanding. Each return to the Mont could open new perspectives, new emotions, and new insights.

As I reflected on my own teaching practice, I realized that the classroom mirrors Mont Sainte-Victoire in many ways. The curriculum may feel repetitive, but every day brings a new constellation of students, materials, spaces, and emotions – that create an event. As teachers, we respond and co-construct meaning within a rich socio material landscape.

I also noticed how much my own environment shapes me as an educator. The classroom materials, the digital tools, the physical space, and the students' voices all influence how I engage and respond. Thinking of the mountain as a symbol of affective resonance, I started to see the importance of engaging with these elements.

This reflection led me to appreciate teaching as a process of co-becoming. Like Cézanne, I am reminded that what may appear repetitive on the surface can, through attentive and affective engagement, become generative. In this light, every lesson becomes an event, every classroom a landscape for co-becoming, and every engagement an invitation to deeper understanding.

CONCLUSION

Events – whether lesson planning, copying exercises, or resource selection – function as minimal units of experience where voices, positions, and materialities converge. Through these interactions, teachers and students alike develop, negotiate, and transform their positions within the classroom's polyphony, illustrating that teaching is not a solitary act but a relational, dialogical, and material process. Each event – the selection of a textbook activity, the production of lesson copies, or the arrangement of classroom materials – functions as a minimal unit where these voices and positions intersect. This chapter approach invites teachers to cultivate perceptual openness: to notice how classroom materials, gestures, spaces, and rhythms resonate with the affective and cognitive dimensions of learning. Matter itself – the textbooks, worksheets, writing tools, or classroom walls – becomes a participant in the pedagogical encounter, shaping and being shaped by the human voices in dialogue. Each interaction generates potential for new meanings, positions, and forms of engagement, allowing teacher and students to co-construct knowledge while negotiating positions.

NOTE

1. https://en.wikipedia.org/wiki/Mont_Sainte-Victoire_(C%C3%A9zanne)

REFERENCES

Bakhtin, M. (1986). *Speech genres and other late essays.* University of Texas Press.

Christensen, M. K., & Weissmann, E. A. (2025). Exploring early career academic teacher identities: Using the audio diary method for reflection and research. *Teaching in Higher Education,* 1–17. https://doi.org/10.1080/13562517.2025.2449655

Diseth, Å. (2025). Reflection notes as a tool for professional development of pre-service psychology teachers. *Reflective Practice,* 1–11. https://doi.org/10.1080/14623943.2025.2504139

Dreyer, L. M. (2015). Reflective journaling: A tool for teacher professional development. *Africa Education Review, 12*(2), 331–344. https://doi.org/10.1080/18146627.2015.1108011

Grossen, M., & Salazar Orvig, A. (2011). Dialogism and dialogicality in the study of the self. *Culture & Psychology, 17*(4), 491–509.

Hermans, H. J. (1996). Voicing the self: From information processing to dialogical interchange. *Psychological Bulletin, 119*(1), 31. https://doi.org/10.1037/0033-2909.119.1.31

Hermans, H. J. M. (2013). The dialogical self in education: Introduction. *Journal of Constructivist Psychology, 26*(2), 81–89. https://doi.org/10.1080/10720537.2013.759018

Hetherington, L., Hardman, M., Noakes, J., & Wegerif, R. (2018). Making the case for a material-dialogic approach to science education. *Studies in Science Education, 54*(2), 141–176.

Kling, I., & Buhl, M. (2025). Applying Q methodology in higher teacher education for pre-service teachers' (self-) reflection, learning and professional development. In *Frontiers in education* (Vol. *10,* p. 1555073). Frontiers Media SA.

Latour, B. (2005). *Reassembling the social: An introduction to actor-network-theory.* Oxford University Press.

Linell, P. (2009). *Rethinking language, mind, and world dialogically.* IAP.

Marková, I., Linell, P., Grossen, M., & Salazar Orvig, A. (2007). *Dialogue in focus groups: Exploring socially shared knowledge.* University of Toronto Press.

Mehto, V., Riikonen, S., Hakkarainen, K., Kangas, K., & Seitamaa-Hakkarainen, P. (2020). Epistemic roles of materiality within a collaborative invention project at a secondary school. *British Journal of Educational Technology, 51*(4), 1246–1261.

Roth, W. M. (2024). Event as minimal unit of analysis. *The Body in Mathematics: Theoretical and Methodological Lenses, 7,* 295.

Tan, A. L., Chang, C. H., & Teng, P. (2015). Tensions and dilemmas in teacher professional development. *Procedia-Social and Behavioral Sciences, 174,* 1583–1591.

Valsiner, J. (2024). *Dynamic semiosis.* Springer.

Wegerif, R. (2013). *Dialogic: Education for the internet age.* Routledge. ISBN-10: 0415536782, ISBN-13: 978-0415536783.

CHAPTER 4

ZONES OF SENSE: PATHWAYS TO TEACHER SELF

ABSTRACT

This chapter explores the teacher's self-awareness by examining how sensory experiences – particularly with soundscapes and photographic images – can deepen pedagogical presence. Drawing from affect theory and dialogical theory, the chapter reframes everyday classroom interactions as multisensory and emotionally charged events that carry potential for transformation. Through the narrative account of vignettes, I investigate how teachers might move beyond habitual, cognitive-centred approaches to embrace a more embodied, situated, and responsive mode of practice. It is an invitation to attentiveness to the minor gestures, silences, and sensory cues that shape the teaching-learning encounter.

Keywords: Teacher self-awareness; sense; emotion; sound; images; dialogical self theory

INTRODUCTION

In an age of increasing standardisation, performance metrics, and instructional efficiency, the relational and affective dimensions of teaching risk being overlooked or minimised (Sabagh et al., 2022). Yet, at its core, teaching is not merely the transmission of knowledge, it is a deeply emotional act (Bergman & Montgomery, 2017; Schratz, 2026).

Teacher Dialogical Self, pages 47–58

doi:10.1108/978-1-80686-957-220261005

Teachers are not neutral conduits of content but are situated beings who engage with students through their voices, gestures, silences, moods, and presences. These subtle, often pre-reflective consciousness (Pacheco & Fossa, 2025) experiences of classroom life – how a teacher pauses before responding, how a glance conveys disappointment or care, how a sound stirs attention or disrupts focus – shape the pedagogical encounter in profound ways. This chapter arises from the need to slow down and attune to the lived, sensory, and affective dimensions of teaching. At a time when educational environments grow increasingly noisy, visually saturated, and emotionally complex (Fernández-Batanero et al., 2021), it becomes strategic for teachers to develop a heightened awareness of their own inner experiences and the atmospheres they co-create with students. Such attentiveness cannot be cultivated solely through rational planning or reflective checklists. It requires new pedagogical practices that recognise the body, emotion, sound, and image as central to how learning unfolds in the classroom (Adamson & Johansson, 2016; Impedovo, 2026). This chapter invites teachers and educators to explore the teaching practices through the pathway of the senses. This focus reframes teaching as a deliberate, situated practice of presence, openness, and ethical relation. It is a call to honour the uncertainties of classroom life, not by controlling them, but by becoming more receptive to the subtle, unfolding dynamics of each moment. In doing so, we open up the possibility for teachers not only to teach more attentively, but to become more attuned to their own becoming – professionally and relationally.

The chapter is structured as follows. It begins with a theoretical discussion of pre-reflective consciousness and multisensory approaches to accessing the teacher's self. To anchor theory in practice, two vignettes drawn from my experience as a teacher-educator are presented. The second section explores how visual and auditory sensoriality can function as mediators between teacher awareness – conceived as an 'inner forest' (Pacheco & Fossa, 2025) – and the external reality of the classroom.

PRE-REFLECTIVE CONSCIOUSNESS: EXCURSUS IN THEORY

Human consciousness has long posed a fundamental challenge to both philosophy and cognitive science. Among its various dimensions, pre-reflective consciousness – the immediate, non-conceptual engagement with the world prior to reflective thought – has garnered particular interest (Pacheco & Fossa, 2025; Valsiner et al., 2021). This form of awareness underlies everyday experience, yet it resists easy articulation due to its deeply subjective nature. As a result, researchers are increasingly called to develop methodological innovations that can evoke such experiences while recognising the constraints imposed by reflection and language (Petitmengin, 2006). Phenomenology, as established by Husserl, offers a robust philosophical framework for examining pre-reflective consciousness by attending to lived experience. At the heart of Husserl's approach (1931, 2005) lies the method of phenomenological reduction, which involves the suspension of judgements and assumptions to access the essential structures of experience. However, this method remains contested, particularly regarding its practical implementation in the study of pre-reflective experience (Moran, 2000). Merleau-Ponty's focus (2013) on embodied perception and Heidegger's notion (2022) of being-in-the-world underscore the idea that pre-reflective experience is not merely mental, but fundamentally grounded in our embodied, situated interactions with the world. Husserl's concept of phenomenological reduction is central to this effort, aiming to bracket preconceived notions and focus on consciousness as it gives itself. Yet this notion is not without ambiguity. Scholars such as Zahavi (2018) have underscored the interpretive complexity of the reduction, particularly in its transcendental orientation – not merely as a method for eliminating bias, but as a means of disclosing the constitutive activity of consciousness itself (Husserl, 2005). Contemporary research includes neurophenomenology and embodied cognition (Gallagher & Zahavi, 2021; Thompson, 2017). These developments highlight the relational and embodied nature of pre-reflective awareness, emphasising that it is always embedded in social, environmental, and corporeal contexts.

Drawing from Pacheco and Fossa (2025), the pre-reflective consciousness, then, designates a form of awareness that precedes deliberate thought or analysis. It refers to the immediate and unmediated encounter with the world, occurring prior to the application of interpretive or conceptual frameworks. The distinction between 'immediate' and 'unmediated' is critical: immediate emphasises the temporal directness of the experience, while unmediated refers to its raw, non-conceptual character. This level of experience is foundational to phenomenological inquiry, as it reveals the primordial ways in which we inhabit the world – not through reflection, but through lived, embodied being. As Pacheco and Fossa (2025, p. 15) conclude their paper: 'The nature of the human consciousness may be understood as an inner forest in which the possibilities of development converge with the set of personal experiences, which nurture the path from which the subject passes his own existence'. In the following, two sections are proposed: the first about multisensory for accessing teacher self with some related account; the second about a focus on sound and image to activate teacher awareness.

IN CLASSROOM: MULTISENSORY FOR ACCESSING TEACHER SELF

The experience of sense reflects a holistic and total experience composed of cognitive but also emotional elements. Vygotsky refers to that aspect of experience as a complex totality, to an affective-cognitive union: 'meaning is only a stone in the building of sense' (Vygotsky, 1934/1986, p. 244). The sense is the indissoluble union of the meaning of the word and the affects, of the cognitive and the emotional aspects of consciousness. So, it is possible to think of sense as the point of contact: from the affective sphere of consciousness to thought and from thought to the affective sphere of consciousness (Curran et al., 2015; Fossa, 2017; Pacheco & Fossa, 2025).

Recent insights from neurophenomenology and affect studies reinforce this perspective by pointing to the multilayered integration of sensory, emotional, and cognitive processes in the construction of self-awareness. As Tossici et al. (2024) explain, emotions and affects emerge not as isolated mental states but through an embodied process of somatic-cognitive integration that engages the entire organism. This integrative system does not operate solely through conscious reflection, but also through affective traces – bodily impressions that surface in response to stimuli such as sound, image, or movement, often before they are cognitively registered. These moments offer access to pre-verbal I-positions, which may remain unvoiced in traditional discursive reflection.

In this chapter, the focus is on examining how sensory experiences – particularly to soundscapes and photographic images, support teachers in accessing pre-reflective dimensions of experience and give form to voices that emerge not in words, but in movement, tone, rhythm, and atmosphere. In this way, reflection becomes not only cognitive but embodied, a dialogical process between sensing and speaking, between silence and interpretation. These practices align with a dialogical conception of identity as fluid, emergent, and negotiated across inner and outer spaces (Impedovo, 2021).

The process of developing teacher self-awareness requires attention not only to cognitive reflection but also to the pre-reflective, embodied dimensions of experience. From the perspective of Dialogical Self Theory (Hermans-Konopka & Hermans, 2010), the self is constituted by a multiplicity of I-positions – internal voices situated in different relational, cultural, and emotional contexts. These positions are not purely cognitive or verbal in nature; they are also bodily lived, shaped through sensation, affect, and the rhythms of everyday experience.

Multisensory methods allow teachers to engage with less dominant I-positions, those often overlooked in institutional or performative roles – and bring them into the field of awareness through gentle, integrative attention. In this framework, teacher identity becomes a process of relational embodiment, were being and becoming are not only thought but also felt, sensed, and enacted. In the following, I use two vignettes – collected in the last academic year from my experience as a teacher educator – to bring examples.

Teacher Self-Account About Multisensory

This vignette about the pressure of meeting exemplifies how different I-positions are not only contextually activated but also somatically experienced:

> *Yesterday morning, I had a meeting with colleagues. I was absorbed in my role, attentive to expectations and external perception. My thoughts were preoccupied with tasks and how others saw me. I felt under pressure.*
>
> *Later, riding home on my bike, I experienced a shift. I noticed the shape of clouds, the sound of birds, and a sense of freedom. I felt more myself.*
>
> *This contrast stayed with me: Why can't I feel this same lightness in my teacher's role? Today, in a new meeting, I tried to engage differently – with more empathy and attentiveness.*
>
> *I was less reactive, yet not fully in touch with that same embodied self I encountered on the bike.*

The experience of the bicycle did not arise from analytical reflection, but from a bodily state of openness – one that enabled a sense of coherence and authenticity not felt in a professional setting. Dialogical Self Theory-helps conceptualise this not as a shift between entirely separate selves, but as a dialogue between internal positions, each carrying its own affective tone, spatial orientation, and embodied presence.

The second vignette is about slowing down between classrooms. It illustrates an exchange between two I-positions within the self: the I-as-responsible-teacher, driven by a sense of duty and urgency, and the I-as-sensory-observer, oriented towards presence, aesthetic appreciation, and embodied awareness.

> *As I moved from one classroom to another, climbing and descending the stairs, I felt the need to slow down. In doing so, I distanced myself from the pressing voice of duty. Slowing down open space to notice the colours, to attune my senses, to seek the gaze and faces of my students.*
>
> *The season revealed its beauty; I felt released from the anxiety of being late and the weight of what might happen. A lightness emerged, a different flavour to the moment. Rapid movements seem to bind me to a pressure that is not mine.*
>
> *Why do I quicken my pace?*
>
> *Again, I tried slowing down, letting the transition between rooms become its own experience.*

The act of slowing down disrupts the dominant voice of obligation, allowing an alternative positioning that reconfigures the relationship to time, space, and others. In Dialogical Self terms, this micro-negotiation reveals how shifting positional dominance can alter affective tone, attentional focus, and ultimately the meaning-making of everyday pedagogical transitions.

IN THE INNER FOREST: SOUND AND IMAGE TO ACTIVATE TEACHER AWARENESS

To deepen teacher self-awareness, it is valuable to explore how visual and auditory sensoriality can act as mediators between the human consciousness-interpreted as an inner forest (Pacheco & Fossa, 2025) and external world.

Drawing on the Dialogical Self Theory (Hermans-Konopka & Hermans, 2010), the self is not a monolithic identity but a dynamic system of I-positions – some verbalised, others evoked pre-reflectively through sensory stimuli. In this context, soundscapes and images offer pathways to access unspoken or unarticulated dimensions of teacher identity, especially those obscured by routine, performance, or professional expectation.

Visual engagement, for example, enables a more embodied form of reflection: visual materials can activate dormant affective responses. As explained in the Theory of dynamic semiosis process the meaning emerges in the unity of schematized and pleromatic experiences (Valsiner, 2024, p. 86):

'The primacy of pleromatic generalisation involves "imageless thought" – the readiness of the human thinking process to create the next concrete form of throught – verbal or image, while in itself not yet being established in either of these form'.

This moment of sign emergence could be linked with the emergence of silent I-positions – those formed in past experiences or marginal perspectives within the self – that may not yet have found language. Such micro-moments of visual disruption bring forward emotional and mnemonic material that invites a dialogical encounter between positions.

Similarly, auditory stimuli – whether ambient sounds, recorded voice, or music – can provoke deeply embodied I-positions tied to spatial, affective, and temporal memories. These sensorial cues open an experiential dialogue between the present moment and prior embodied states, offering a shift away from purely discursive introspection. As Leavy (2015) and Rogers (2020) demonstrate, symbolic and aesthetic forms of expression facilitate emotional integration by bypassing the rational filter of language.

As a practical example of reflective exercise, we introduce here an image from the Musée de Cluny, La Dame à la Licorne (see Fig. 4).[1] I ask the readers not to interpret but to attune to what emerged – visually, emotionally, bodily.

For some, this image may evoke maternal presence, for others, a sense of unattainability, or a call for gentleness. For me, it activated a sense of calm, serenity and recall for a past serenity. These evocations are close to the pre-reflective activations of different I-positions: 'I-as-caring', 'I-as-sensible' These voices became accessible not through speech but through aesthetic resonance (Impedovo, 2025). This sensory approach, when framed dialogically,

Fig. 4. Hearing (3.70 m × 2.90 m) by Didier Descouens – Own Work, Public Domain https://commons.wikimedia.org/w/index.php?curid=115192710. *Source:* This file is licenced under the Creative Commons Attribution-Share Alike 4.0 International licence.

enables teachers to reposition themselves in ways that include affective, intuitive, and non-linear ways of knowing.

Rather than viewing reflection as a rational exercise, this practice recognises reflection as a multimodal, relational encounter with the self – where the teacher's internal forest is traversed through light, sound, silence, and emotional texture.

Listening to the Unseen: Soundscapes for Affective Rhythms

This attentiveness to sound invites us to reimagine the pedagogical self through a dialogical lens (Hermans-Konopka & Hermans, 2010), where inner voices are activated not only through speech or reflection, but through auditory and embodied presence. The teacher's practice of listening cultivates a dynamic positioning: 'I-as-caregiver', or 'I-as-silenced', may all be called into dialogue through shifts in the sonic environment. In the following, an illustrative vignette about one teaching practice.

> *This morning, before the bell, I arrived earlier than usual to sit in silence within the classroom. I listen – not to language, but to the layered soundscape of space: the faint hum of ventilation, birdsong through cracked windows, the knock of movement next door.*
>
> *During lessons, I attune to more subtle shifts: the rising excitement in a student's voice, the heavy silence after a question, the sonic contours of laughter, unease, or resistance.*
>
> *When a student goes quietly, I don't intervene immediately. Instead, I honour silence as a space of potential.*

Exploring classroom life through its sonic dimension offers a vital alternative to vision- and language-dominated conceptions of pedagogy (Ahern, 2018; Shoemaker & Werner, 2020). The acoustic textures of schooling – buzzing lights, hallway footsteps, whispering students, the rhythm of writing, or even shared silence – create a soundscape that shapes emotional and relational meaning (Hytonen-Ng et al., 2022). These sonic presences, often relegated to the margins, participate in the formation of classroom atmospheres and intersubjective dialogue. A bell may signal routine or anxiety; a change in tone may soothe or alienate. These affective modulations structure the emotional grammar of teaching and learning (Verstraete & Hoegaerts, 2017).

Crucially, sound in the classroom is not neutral. What is heard, ignored, or dismissed shapes which voices within the self and among others are legitimised. Selective listening, as Ceraso (2018) reminds us, reveals underlying patterns of attention and exclusion.

Silence, in this light, becomes a pedagogical position. As Massumi (2011, 2016) suggests, silence is a speculative space not yet shaped by meaning, yet rich with possibility. Minor gestures such as allowing silence to linger, or acknowledging the tremor in a student's voice, create space for transformation.

Through silence, the teacher may hear the emergence of new positions: 'I-as-vulnerable', 'I-as-not-knowing', or 'I-as-trusting'. Sound, in this expanded sense, becomes a vibrational terrain in which teacher and student selves co-evolve, and reposition. Here, listening becomes a form of presence, and the body – always situated, sensing, and responding – emerges as both listener and voice in the unfolding story of teaching and learning.

Photography, Affect, and Teacher Self-Awareness

Photography speaks a language rich in nuance, ambiguity, and multiplicity. A single photograph can carry multiple meanings at once, acting as a symbolic container where personal memories, sensations, and interpretations accumulate.

> *During a routine tidy-up at the end of the semester, I noticed a photograph tacked to the far corner of the classroom bulletin board.*
>
> *I remember that day: the fatigue, my doubt about whether the workshop had landed. And yet, the image tells another story – a relational one. In this capture, I see warmth, connection, and shared engagement.*
>
> *The photo becomes more than a memory. It's a mirror. It reflects not just what happened, but how it felt, how it moved, how it connected. Later, I printed the image and placed it in his planning diary.*
>
> *Not as a trophy, but as a quiet reminder: sometimes, the most meaningful moments of teaching are the ones we don't immediately see.*

This vignette highlights the disjunction between lived experience in the moment and its retrospective reinterpretation through material traces – in this case, a photograph. In pedagogical terms, it demonstrates how artefacts can act as mediators of memory and meaning, reframing self-evaluations that may be clouded by fatigue or doubt. The shift from an internal narrative of uncertainty to a recognition of relational depth aligns with theories of reflective reframing and affective witnessing in teacher development. The photograph functions here not as mere documentation, but as a dialogical partner – opening a conversation between the I-in-the-moment and the I-in-retrospect – allowing the teacher to access dimensions of the encounter that were 'unseen' in real time.

Photography gives form to the invisible; it allows abstract or unspoken aspects of experience – such as affect, memory, or relational dynamics – to become visible and discussable (Wilson, 2020). As Ferraro and Tamborini (2021) suggest, this act of visual abstraction supports psychological reflection, inviting educators to step outside the immediate intensity of daily classroom life and reconsider it with openness and care. It mediates reflection, triggers emotional resonance, and facilitates deeper understanding of self and other.

DISCUSSION

At the heart of teaching lies a paradox: while much of classroom life depends on structure, predictability, and planning, the most meaningful moments often emerge from uncertainty. Uncertainty can be a site of ethical and relational becoming – a threshold that disrupts automatic responses and creates space for genuine presence and responsiveness. When teachers stay open to the uncertainty, they cultivate an attentiveness that cannot be reduced to instructional techniques. They create conditions where something new – unexpected, relational, affective – might emerge. One way to remain present to these moments is by rethinking routine not as mechanical repetition, but as an intentional and embodied practice. Routine, in its conventional sense, often becomes automatic, carried out without reflection. A shift on the sensorially could transform the ordinary into the meaningful by grounding action in awareness, attention, and care. In this transformation, the same gesture – taking attendance, starting a lesson, giving feedback – shifts from being merely procedural to becoming relational and affectively charged. This transformation means asking: What if I approached this moment not as a task to be completed, but as an opportunity to connect? What if silence was not a pause to be filled, but a space of shared waiting? What if the way I begin each class could become a collective grounding, an opening to shared experience? This reframing does not demand additional time or elaborate design – it asks for intentional presence. This invitation means becoming more attuned to what is unfolding in the moment – the subtle shifts in student affect, the emotional weight of a topic, the resonance or dissonance in a classroom's atmosphere. In this frame, uncertainty becomes a generative companion, not an obstacle. In doing so, we make room for what truly matters: the formation of relationships, the unfolding of understanding, and the collective making of meaning.

NOTE

1. By Wikipedia: The Lady and the Unicorn (French: La Dame à la licorne) is the modern title given to a series of six tapestries created in the style of millefleurs ('1,000 flowers') and woven in Flanders from wool and silk, from designs ('cartoons') drawn in Paris around 1500. The set is on display in the Musée de Cluny in Paris.

REFERENCES

Adamson, M., & Johansson, M. (2016). Compositions of professionalism in counselling work: An embodied and embedded intersectionality framework. *Human Relations, 69*(12), 2201–2223.

Ahern, K. F. (2018). Understanding learning spaces sonically, soundscaping evaluations of place. *Computers and Composition, 48*, 22–33. https://doi.org/10.1016/j.compcom.2018.03.007

Bergman, C., & Montgomery, N. (2017). *Joyful militancy: Building thriving resistance in toxic times.* AK Press.

Ceraso, S. (2018). *Sounding composition: Multimodal pedagogies for embodied listening.* University of Pittsburgh Press. https://muse.jhu.edu/book/60438

Curran, T., Hill, A. P., Appleton, P. R., Vallerand, R. J., & Standage, M. (2015). The psychology of passion: A meta-analytical review of a decade of research on intrapersonal outcomes. *Motivation and Emotion, 39*(5), 631–655.

Fernández-Batanero, J. M., Román-Graván, P., Reyes-Rebollo, M. M., & Montenegro-Rueda, M. (2021). Impact of educational technology on teacher stress and anxiety: A literature review. *International Journal of Environmental Research and Public Health, 18*(2), 548. https://doi.org/10.3390/ijerph18020548

Ferraro, A., & Tamborini, M. (2021). Abstraction in contemporary visual culture as an interplay between imagination, image and scientific knowledge. *Visual Resources, 37*(2), 139–154. https://doi.org/10.1080/01973762.2023.2186768

Fossa, P. (2017). Pleromatization, phyisiognomization and metaphoricity: A theoretical articulation of sense making processes of Valsiner, Werner and McNeill. *Psicologia USP, 28,* 93–101.

Gallagher, S., & Zahavi, D. (2021). *The phenomenological mind.* Routledge.

Heidegger, M. (2022). *Being and time.* Lushena Books.

Hermans-Konopka, A., & Hermans, H. J. (2010). *The dynamic features of love: Changes in self and motivation.*

Husserl, E. (1931). *Ideas: General introduction to pure phenomenology.* Macmillan.

Husserl, E. (2005). *Phantasy, image consciousness, and memory* (pp. 1898–1925). Springer.

Hytonen-Ng, E., Pihlainen, K., Ng, K., & Karna, E. (2022). Sounds of learning: Soundscapes - Teacher perceptions of acoustic environments in finland's open plan classrooms. *Issues in Educational Research, 32*(4), 1421–1440. https://search.informit.org/doi/10.3316/informit.806801987450716

Impedovo, M. (2026). Affectivity as a pedagogical approach for transforming teaching-learning relationships. In A. Dania & et M. Impedovo (Eds.), *Affectivity as pedagogy in the classroom interdisciplinary approaches to relationship-based practice in education.* Routledge.

Impedovo, M. A. (2021). *Identity and teacher professional development: A reflective, collaborative and agentive learning journey.* SPRINGER BRIEF. ISBN 978-3-030-71367-6.

Impedovo, M. (2025). Mirroring the self through Hamlet affective aesthetic experience. *Integrative Psychological and Behavioral Science, 59*(3), 1–16.

Leavy, P. (2015). Methods meets art: Arts-based research practice. *Forum for Qualitative Social Research, 16*(1), 19.

Massumi, B. (2011). *Semblance and event. Activist philosophy and the occurent arts.* MIT Press.

Massumi, B. (2016). Such as it is: A short essay in extreme realism. *Body & Society, 21*(1), 115–127.

Merleau-Ponty, M. (2013). *Phenomenology of perception.* Routledge.

Moran, D. (2000). *Introduction to phenomenology.* Routledge.

Pacheco, C., & Fossa, P. (2025). Phenomenological mapping: A method for understanding pre-reflective consciousness. *Integrative Psychological and Behavioral Science, 59*(1), 6.

Petitmengin, C. (2006). Describing one's subjective experience in the second person: An interview method for the science of consciousness. *Phenomenology and the Cognitive Sciences, 5*(3), 229–269.

Rogers, C. (2020). Necessary connections: 'Feelings photographs' in criminal justice research. *Methodological Innovations, 13*(2). (Original work published 2020). https://doi.org/10.1177/2059799120925255

Sabagh, Z., Hall, N. C., Saroyan, A., & Trépanier, S. G. (2022). Occupational factors and faculty well-being: Investigating the mediating role of need frustration. *The Journal of Higher Education, 93*(4), 559–584. https://doi.org/10.1080/00221546.2021.2004810

Schratz, M. (2026). Introduction to affectivity as pedagogy in the classroom. In A. Dania & M. Impedovo (Eds.), *Affectivity as pedagogy in the classroom interdisciplinary approaches to relationship-based practice in education.* Routledge.

Shoemaker, D., & Werner, K. (2020). Listening and becoming through sound: Audio autoethnographic collaboration as critical communication pedagogy. *Review of Communication, 20*(4), 355–366. https://doi.org/10.1080/15358593.2020.1819557

Thompson, E. (2017). *Waking self and consciousness in neuroscience, meditation, and philosophy.* Columbia University Press.

Tossici, G., Zurloni, V., Marsico, G., & De Luca Picione, R. (2024). The role of affectivity in pre-reflective experience. The contributions of neuroscientific, psychoanalytical and developmental perspectives. *Human Arenas,* 1–19.

Valsiner, J. (2024). *Dynamic semiosis.* Springer.

Valsiner, J., Tsuchimoto, T., Ozawa, I., Chen, X., & Horie, K. (2021). The intermodal Pre-Construction Method (IMPreC): Exploring hyper-generalization. *Human Arenas, 6*(4), 1–19.

Verstraete, P., & Hoegaerts, J. (2017). Educational soundscapes: Tuning in to sounds and silences in the history of education. *Paedagogica Historica, 53*(5), 491–497. https://doi.org/10.1080/00309230.2017.1358291

Vygotsky, L. S. (1934/1986). *Thought and language.* The MIT Press.

Wilson, A. N. (2020). Learning to see with Deleuze: Understanding affective responses in image-viewer research assemblages. *Qualitative Research, 21*(6), 906–922. https://doi.org/10.1177/1468794120946979

Zahavi, D. (2018). *Phenomenology: The basics.* Routledge.

CHAPTER 5

EXPLORING THE TEACHER BODILY SELF

ABSTRACT

Drawing from affect theory and dialogical self-theory, using narrative account, the chapter examines how bodily movement, gesture, and posture serve not only as indicators of internal emotional states but also as relational acts that shape pedagogical encounters. Emphasis is placed on the body's capacity to affect and be affected, highlighting its role as a site of ongoing transformation, communication, and becoming. This chapter is proposed as a 'walking chapter' – not only a metaphor but also an invitation to engage with this text in motion.

Keywords: Teacher; bodily self; I-positions; body; meaning; affect theory

INTRODUCTION

Although interest in embodied learning has grown across multiple educational perspectives (Lakoff & Johnson, 1999), the teacher's body remains marginal in mainstream professional development discourse. Even as learner-centred pedagogies increasingly acknowledge the importance of affect, movement, and bodily presence in the learning process (Shapiro & Stolz, 2019), teachers are still often framed as neutral. Policy frameworks, teacher training curricula, and classroom observation tools tend to prioritise cognitive skills, instructional strategies, and verbal communication, while

Teacher Dialogical Self, pages 59–70

doi:10.1108/978-1-80686-957-220261006

giving limited attention to posture, gesture, physical presence, or affective regulation.

Yet teaching is inherently an embodied act. It requires ongoing physical engagement, emotional investment, and rich layers of non-verbal interaction, all mediated through the body (Impedovo, 2024; Morris, 2017). Building on scholarships in embodiment (Mandalaki & Fotaki, 2020; Snowber, 2016) and affect (Zembylas, 2007) and dialogical approaches to self and professional practice (Hermans & Gieser, 2012), this chapter advocates for repositioning the teacher's body as a site for meaning making. By engaging the body as a narrative and reflective resource, teachers can cultivate more nuanced forms of self-awareness, enriching both their practice and their connections with learners: embodiment as 'experiential beings in motion, both inscribed and inscribing subjectivities' (Ellingson, 2017, p. 2).

This chapter is proposed as a 'walking chapter'. The 'walking chapter' is not only a metaphor but also an invitation to engage with this text in motion – reading while walking or walking before reading – as thinkers and educators have done for centuries. From the peripatetic teaching of Aristotle's Lyceum to the reflective ambulations of Rousseau (1995) and the observational strolls of the flâneur, walking has been a recognised modality for reflection, dialogue, and the cultivation of insight. In this sense, the act of walking does more than accompany the reading; it shapes it. The rhythm of steps, the shifting light, and the ambient sounds all become part of the chapter's meaning.

Contemporary research on embodied cognition reinforces this historical intuition, showing that physical movement can enhance creativity, learning, and relational attunement (Markman, 2020; O'Mara, 2019). To walk while reading – or to let a walk precede and follow the reading – allows the ideas here to settle not only in the mind but also in the body. The physical act of moving through space encourages a slowing down, a heightened awareness of sensation, and an openness to the subtle interplay between thought and environment. In this way, the 'walking chapter' aligns with an embodied mode of inquiry, where pedagogy is felt in breath, gait, and pause as much as it is reasoned on the page.

The chapter is structured as follows. First, a theoretical perspective on the self as fundamentally situated in the body is introduced, accompanied by practical examples of its application. The two subsequent sections draw on reflective accounts and vignette (Langer, 2016). The first illustrates how habitual patterns of action not only shape the ways in which teachers approach their work but also influence how they relate to themselves and to others. The second account demonstrates how dialogical processes unfold not only through language, but also through bodily awareness and spatial movement. The third account illustrates how bodily awareness and movement help to find a new reconfiguration into the space and meanings.

THEORETICAL ASPECTS: THE SELF AS FUNDAMENTALLY SITUATED IN THE BODY

The Dialogical Self Theory, as proposed by Hermans and colleagues (Hermans & Kempen, 1993; Hermans & Hermans-Konopka, 2010), foregrounds the idea that the self is not a unitary construct but a dynamic multiplicity of 'I-positions' in dialogue within the individual and between individuals. While traditionally framed in terms of psychological and linguistic interactions, recent developments have emphasised the embodied nature of these dialogical processes, arguing that the body is not merely the vessel for self-dialogue, but an active, expressive site of dialogical positioning. From a developmental standpoint, early bodily interactions – such as eye contact, mutual gaze, and joint attention – form the foundation for proto-dialogs between infants and caregivers (Hermans & Hermans-Konopka, 2010). These pre-verbal exchanges suggest that dialogue emerges from bodily attunement before it becomes linguistic, laying the groundwork for internal I-positions that are both socially and corporeally situated.

Hermans (2001) further draws attention to the spatial character of the self, wherein bodily movement through physical space (e.g., near/far, up/down) is mirrored by metaphorical positioning of self-voices (e.g., dominant/submissive, active/passive). This underscores how bodily movement informs the cognitive-emotional structure of dialogical self-experience. The implication is that self-dialogue is not only a matter of inner speech but also of embodied action and orientation. Empirical research supports this connection. Raggatt (2000) found that individuals associate different parts of the body with specific I-positions, often along gendered lines: for example, women were more likely to associate positive self-voices with facial features and negative ones with lower-body features, while men showed the inverse. These findings suggest that bodily self-image is internalized into dialogical structures, influencing how individuals engage in inner conversations.

Moreover, critiques from within dialogical theory have called for a more integrated view of the corporeal self. Cresswell and Baerveldt (2009) argue for a Bakhtinian account of embodiment, which situates bodily responsiveness at the core of dialogical interaction. In this framework, the body is not passive but responsive and anticipatory, shaping the very conditions of meaning-making in dialogical relations. In fact, Cresswell & Baerveldt highlight the necessity of more fully integrating the notion of the embodied self into dialogical theory. Bakhtin conceives of dialogue as an ontological condition of all that holds meaning and significance – embedded in the very fabric of lived human experience, rather than confined to the internal processes of the individual mind (Bakhtin, 1984). Thus, his vision of dialogue resists both individualistic and disembodied readings. In contrast, many contemporary approaches to dialogue continue to emphasise a notion of the core self as an internally located and context-independent entity. Emphasising the embodied self, however, entails recognising the intricate interweaving of biological, social, cultural, and historical dimensions. From this perspective, the body is not merely a personal possession but a profoundly social and situated entity, actively participating in the co-construction of meaning. Furthermore, Bakhtin's (1984) concept of the 'grotesque body' emphasises the deep connection between language, meaning, and the body. This idea presents an 'upside-down' view that challenges the separation between bodily existence and its social and historical context. By breaking down these boundaries, the body can be understood as existing at the crossroads between the private and public spheres – it is both a personal and a social expression of human life.

The self is thus not located in a single, fixed place but in multiplicity – in the very world we inhabit, in what we know through our participation, and in what we become as part of that world.

The growing integration of embodiment into Dialogical Self Theory marks a shift towards understanding the self as fundamentally situated in the body, both in developmental origins and in ongoing psychological functioning. Rens van Loon (2024) suggest describing and experiencing our bodies as an I-body, as a 'corps sujet' (body subject) This embodied perspective enhances our comprehension of dialogical learning, particularly in educational contexts where bodily presence, gesture, and space play essential roles in meaning negotiation.

Looking at the Body as the Theatre of Emotion

The following proposal starts from the idea that 'in order to think we have first to feel' (Valsiner, 2024, p. XI). In a possible teacher education workshop, I propose to use the starting question *What do we feel looking at this picture?* as an opening invitation to the teacher students to engage with a picture.

The starting question invites the students to shift the focus from what the image represents (cognitive interpretation) to how it is experienced (emotional, sensory, relational resonance). By foregrounding feelings rather than immediate interpretation, the activity created space for sensory, emotional, and embodied responses to emerge without the constraints of predetermined frameworks. This starting question of the workshop for teacher training is ideally posed before offering any contextual information, allowing participants to pause, look closely, and remain with their first impressions. The activity positions the image not merely as an illustration but as a stimulus for first, individual and after, collective meaning-making, noting points of convergence and divergence. This process mirrors the iterative nature of reflective practice (Schön, 2017), where awareness is revisited and refined over time. It also aligns with sensory ethnography approaches (Pink, 2015), recognising that affective and embodied engagement can be as revealing as verbal analysis. With the confrontation with the picture, the task invites students to value the immediacy of felt experience as a legitimate and generative dimension of teacher learning.

For this example, the selected picture is the Capitoline Venus (Fig. 5), a renowned classical sculpture representing the goddess, Venus.

Fig. 5. The Capitoline Venus (Capitoline Museums).[1] By © José Luiz Bernardes Ribeiro, CC BY-SA 4.0, https://commons.wikimedia.org/w/index.php?curid=53996071. *Source:* This file is licenced under the Creative Commons Attribution-Share Alike 4.0 International licence.

The statue in the image is a Roman marble copy of the famous ancient Greek sculpture 'Aphrodite of Knidos' (also known as Venus of Knidos), originally created by the sculptor Praxiteles in the fourth century BCE. This particular representation is one of many Roman copies made after the lost Greek original. The sculpture depicts the goddess Aphrodite (Venus in Roman mythology) just before or after bathing, covering herself modestly with one hand – a pose that came to be known as the 'Venus Pudica' (modest Venus) type. The draped object beside her is often interpreted as a water jar and clothing, reinforcing the bath context. This statue was revolutionary in antiquity as one of the first life-sized representations of the nude female form in Greek art, and it has had a profound influence on the Western canon of beauty and the representation of femininity. The Capitoline Venus embodies ideals of beauty, femininity, and classical artistic values that have deeply influenced Western art and culture. Its depiction invites viewers to reflect on historical conceptions of the body, aesthetics, and identity, making it a rich visual stimulus for discussions around perception, embodiment, and cultural symbolism – key themes in psychology and education.

My related narrative account is here proposed as example of interpretation:

The statue, timeless and unmoving, evokes not only the grace of classical beauty but a deeply embodied presence. Her posture – modest yet self-assured – invites me into a silent dialogue. One hand shields her body while the other rests gently, suggesting both vulnerability and dignity. The cool marble surface belies the warmth of human emotion we project onto her: shyness, surprize, perhaps even resistance. I feel the tension between exposure and concealment.

In her stillness, she stirs something within us: a recognition of the body's expressive power, of how emotion takes form in flesh, in gesture, in silence. The presence of someone else is intense: Maybe an isolated man? Or a group of people? I feel a little uneasy for her too, catcher in her intimate of her toilette. I am looking at her too. Looking at her, I see the echo of our efforts to inhabit our bodies with integrity – to hold space for emotion, memory, and presence.

As expressed in the narrative account, the woman in Fig. 5 may reveal her internal state through posture and gesture, while also indicating her resistance to the presence of others: the body engages with other bodies by staying open to change and influence; such openness constitutes the foundation of dialogical interaction (Shirvani & Shirvani, 2023). This embodied sensitivity extends beyond the individual to the relational field: our bodies are always in relation with the worlds they inhabit just as those worlds inhabit our bodies (Field-Springer, 2019; Katzman, 2015).

As Damasio (1999) emphasises, emotions use 'the body as their theatre' (p. 51), underscoring the inherently embodied nature of emotional experience. Human interaction is saturated with non-verbal forms of dialogue – including facial expressions, gestures, tone of voice, gaze, posture, and bodily proximity (Lyle et al., 2024). These forms of embodied communication are fundamental to how we express, negotiate, and co-construct meaning. Artistic modalities such as dance, music, and performance also serve as powerful vehicles of dialogical exchange (Impedovo, 2025).

BODILY PATTERNS AND THEIR PEDAGOGICAL IMPLICATIONS

The following reflective accounts, from my collected qualitative experiences as a teacher educator (Attia & Edge, 2017), illustrates how habitual patterns of action shape not only how teachers approach their work, but also how they relate to themselves and to others.

> *I am driven by tasks and staying busy. I feel most alive when I am doing something, completing tasks, or following a rhythm. My need to do influences my attitudes, values, reactions, and judgements.*
>
> *Sometimes I run on autopilot, driven by habits. I focus so much on tasks that I become blind to people's emotional needs or relationships. When strong feelings come up, I escape into movement instead of facing them.*
>
> *Stopping for a long time to analyse a situation more deeply often feels less productive than simply moving on.*
>
> *During the teaching, I cannot continuously ask questions, assign tasks, distribute roles, move around the classroom, always busy and in movement… I need to slow down and wait, engaging with them differently otherwise I will miss the real exchange I am looking for.*

As Merleau-Ponty (1945/1986) reminds us, 'our body is in the world as the heart is in the organism' (p. 203); it does not merely occupy space but animate and sustains our participation in the world. Teaching inhabits roles, express values, and co-create meaning through their gestures, posture, tone, and rhythms of engagement. This awareness becomes particularly relevant when teaching styles grounded in task-orientation meet the unpredictable, emotionally charged realities of student interaction. In the account, I recognise that the constant drive to assign tasks or fill the space with activity may hinder authentic connection with students. The shift from doing to being – from controlling the exchange to entering into it – is a movement towards what Buber (1923/1958) terms the 'I-Thou' relation: an encounter in which the other is not objectified but engaged with in full presence. Experiential learning, in this light, involves more than action; it requires the unlearning of habitual reactions. This stepping requires vulnerability – a willingness to pause, feel, and relate in the moment. As Hycner (1993) emphasises, the dialogical space arises in between persons who are open to encounter. But this also applies within the self, where internal multiplicity, including embodied tensions – can be acknowledged rather than overridden. Emotions, as Damasio (1999) point out, are not abstract phenomena; they manifest through movement, tension, and energy. To access this form of knowing is to reconnect with what the body remembers, and the mind may deny (Allen, 1995). Understanding these sensations – the urge to move, the restlessness when facing emotions, the pressure to act – offers insights for transformation.

GENERATING NEW MEANING THROUGH THE BODY

Through bodily gestures, postures, and even physiological responses, teachers participate in an ongoing dialogue – not only with students but with themselves. Yet, as the following vignette illustrates, this bodily dialogue often remains unexamined, even though it is central to the construction of professional identity and relational meaning.

> *I was on the phone with a student. She didn't do well on the test because she didn't study enough. But she blamed my system of evaluation instead. I felt frustrated and found myself gesticulating as I tried to explain my side.*
>
> *I asked myself: 'Why do I feel the need to gesture at this moment? since she can't even see me on the phone. I resisted the urge to gesticulate and instead focused on staying calm.*
>
> *That changed the conversation: it became more productive. I realized that her failure wasn't only due to a lack of effort, but also other reasons. We talked and found a constructive way forward. I realized, at the end of the call, that I often use gestures when feeling challenged – even when unseen.*
>
> *Maybe my Italian cultural background stepped in, but I felt the emotional tensions in my gestures.*

My spontaneous gesturing, though invisible to the student on the phone, became a powerful cue of internal emotional tension – a bodily enactment of self-defence and frustration. An embodied reflexivity as a 'mutual and reciprocal exchange of knowledge, perception, and bodily actions in each other's presence' (Field-Springer, 2019, p. 4). Engaging from and with the sensing and perceiving body allows teachers to access a level of awareness in which learning becomes visible – not as an abstract process, but as a lived and embodied one. Bodily experience is not merely a background to teaching; it is part of how meaning is made, how relationships are navigated, and how professional knowledge is formed.

Teaching situations, when unpacked, reveal the entanglement of cognition, emotion, and gesture in the lived experience of the classroom. The body, then, is not only where we experience tension or fatigue – it is where we feel resonance, resistance, and connection. It is a relational interface, showing, perceiving, and enacting the way we are with ourselves and with others – also when mediated by technology (Impedovo & Gadille, 2021). In this sense, professional learning involves a growing attunement to our bodily selves, enabling us to become more ethical, responsive, and present teacher and teacher educators. By paying attention to the embodied self, we open up new possibilities for teaching as a co-constructed, situated, and deeply human practice.

RECONFIGURATION OF THE SELF WITHIN INTERACTIONAL CONTEXTS

The following reflective vignette illustrates how dialogical processes unfold not only through language, but also through bodily awareness and spatial movement.

> *This morning, I decided not to give in to haste, to feel my body, and to try to observe when a certain emotion would arise in response to the colleague's attitude.*
>
> *My body reacted with some changes in posture, and several times I stepped away from the meeting to look at the sky or the flowers in the courtyard, or simply by making a brief phone call.*
>
> *While I was listening, I also tried to observe his bodily reactions... His tone of voice was loud and strong, his body tense, his face strained. The same thing happens to me too.*

The positions – 'I-as-hurried professional', 'I-in-relation-to-the-colleague' – emerged not in isolation but through a process of internal dialogical movement, shaped by external cues and somatic responses. The attention to bodily posture and gesture reflects a meta-position (Hermans & Gieser, 2012) – a vantage point from which different I-positions are evaluated, and (re)organised in the moment of interaction.

Importantly, the body serves here as more than an instrument of regulation; it is an active medium of engagement. Stepping away from the meeting, looking at the sky, or observing the physical environment function as embodied repositioning acts. These movements mark a shift not only in physical space but in relational orientation and emotional tone. Through these acts, there is an open space for reflective processing.

Furthermore, the recognition of the colleague's bodily tension – 'his tone of voice was loud... his face strained' – echoes the narrator's own experiences, revealing a moment of affective resonance. Dialogical positioning includes embodied responses, gestures, and rhythms of presence that allow for more nuanced forms of meaning-making.

Thus, this narrative accounts exemplifies how embodied awareness enhances capacity to navigate affective tensions with greater flexibility and self-other recognition. The body's role is not merely to express pre-existing positions, but to actively mediate the emergence, transformation, and reconfiguration of the self within interactional contexts.

DISCUSSION

This chapter calls for a teacher's professional development that embraces not only ideas but also presence – one that recognises gesture, silence, rhythm, and emotional labour as essential to the formation of the self and the co-construction of meaning within educational contexts. The implications extend to the body's affective engagement, which both shapes and is shaped by social interactions (Dernikos et al., 2020). Affect operates as a relational force, a pre-cognitive intensity that circulates between bodies and frames the way meaning is collaboratively produced in each moment. Embracing this perspective transforms the classroom into an affective field – a space where each voice and body either finds resonance or encounters dissonance (Gravett, 2023). Within these dynamic, bodily gestures, emotional tensions, and silences are not mere background noise to be controlled but rather meaningful contributions to both internal and external dialogs. For instance, a student's posture or gaze may convey resistance, curiosity, or vulnerability, prompting specific teacher responses that reposition the teacher's own subjectivities, such as 'I-as-supportive', 'I-as-authority', or 'I-as-insecure'.

These affective exchanges continuously modulate each individual's capacity to act, reflect, and connect (Gregg & Seigworth, 2020). Furthermore, classroom interactions are embedded within social hierarchies and historical tensions that influence which voices and bodies are heard, welcomed, or marginalised (Juvonen & Kolehmainen, 2018). These positions could be actively addressed through intentional and care-focused pedagogical practices – helping us to focus on 'what matters' (Snowber, 2012, p. 122) in our teaching and learning lives.

CONCLUSION

In this chapter, we have broadly explored how the focus on the teacher body offers an insight into the dynamic construction of the dialogical self. The internalisation of embodied experience emerges not only as a conceptual metaphor but as a lived process that shapes how teachers relate to themselves, their students, and their pedagogical practice. The voicing of I-positions, when accompanied by an awareness of the body, expands the repertoire of possible meanings one can attribute to past and present experiences. Thus, the body becomes a gateway to a fuller range of self-narratives, inclusive of the affirming and the difficult aspects of professional identity.

NOTE

1. From Wikipedia: The Capitoline Venus is a type of statue of Venus, specifically one of several Venus Pudica (modest Venus) types, of which several examples exist. The type ultimately derives from the Aphrodite of Cnidus. The Capitoline Venus and her variants are recognisable from the position of the arms – standing after a bath, Venus begins to cover her breasts with her right hand, and her groin with her left hand.

REFERENCES

Allen, P. (1995). *Art is a way of knowing*. Shambhala.

Attia, M., & Edge, J. (2017). Be(com) ing a reflexive researcher: A developmental approach to research methodology. *Open Review of Educational Research, 4*(1), 33–45. https://doi.org/10.1080/23265507.2017.1300068

Bakhtin, M. (1984). *Rabelais and his world*. Indiana University Press.

Buber, M. (1923/1958). *I and thou*. Charles Scribner ad Sons.

Cresswell, J., & Baerveldt, J. (2009). Materiality matters: Towards a reformulation of the dialogical self along Bakhtinian lines. In T. Teo, P. Stenner, A. Rutherford, E. Park, & C. Baerveldt (Eds.), *Varieties of theoretical psychology* (pp. 316–325). Captus Press.

Damasio, A. (1999). *The feeling of what happens: Body, emotion and the making of consciousness*. Vintage Books.

Dernikos, B., Lesko, N., McCall, S. D., & Niccolini, A. (2020). *Mapping the affective turn in education. Theory, research, and pedagogies*. Routledge.

Ellingson, L. L. (2017). *Embodiment in qualitative research*. Routledge.

Field-Springer, K. (2019). Reflexive embodied ethnography with applied sensibilities: Methodological reflections on involved qualitative research. *Qualitative Research, 20*(2), 194–212. https://doi.org/10.1177/1468794119841835

Gravett, K. (2023). *Relational pedagogies: Connections and mattering in higher education*. Bloomsbury.

Hermans, H. J., & Kempen, H. J. (1993). *The dialogical self: Meaning as a movement*. Academic Press.

Hermans, H. J. M., & Gieser, T. (Eds.). (2012). *Handbook of dialogical self theory*. Cambridge University Press.

Hermans, H. J. M., & Hermans-Konopka, A. (2010). *Dialogical self theory: Positioning and counter-positioning in a globalizing society*. Cambridge University Press.

Hycner, R. (1993). *Between person and person*. The Gestalt Journal Press Inc.

Impedovo, M., & Gadille, M. (2021). Embodiment in knots of sense-making between learning physical and virtual configurations. *E-Learning and Digital Media, 18*(2), 145–162.

Impedovo, M. A. (2024). Intersubjectivity, materiality, and virtuality: What COVID-19 day-life taught a teacher about navigating a global crisis. *Cultural and Pedagogical Inquiry, 16*(2), 64–67.

Impedovo, M. (2025). Mirroring the self through Hamlet affective aesthetic experience. *Integrative Psychological and Behavioral Science, 59*(3), 1–16.

Juvonen, T., & Kolehmainen, M. (Eds.). (2018). *Affective inequalities in intimate relationships*. Routledge.

Katzman, E. R. (2015). Embodied reflexivity: Knowledge and the body in professional practice. In B. Green & N. Hopwood (Eds.), *The body in professional practice, learning and education* (pp. 157–172). Springer.

Lakoff, G., & Johnson, M. (1999). *Philosophy in the flesh: The embodied mind and its challenge to Western thought*. Basic Books.

Langer, P. C. (2016). The research vignette: Reflexive writing as interpretative representation of qualitative inquiry—A methodological proposition. *Qualitative Inquiry, 22*(9), 735–744. https://doi.org/10.1177/1077800416658066

Lyle, E., Ryu, J. Y., & Snowber, C. N. (2024). Embodied reflexivity through the arts: An introduction. *Qualitative Inquiry, 30*(2), 119–123. https://doi.org/10.1177/10778004231219806

Mandalaki, E., & Fotaki, M. (2020). The bodies of the commons: Towards a relational embodied ethics of the commons. *Journal of Business Ethics, 166*(4), 745–760.

Markman, H. C. (2020). Embodied attunement and participation. *Journal of the American Psychoanalytic Association, 68*(5), 807–834.

Merleau-Ponty, M. (1945/1986). *Phenomenology of perception* (Trans. C. Smith). Routledge and Kegan Paul.

Gregg, M., & Seigworth, G. J. (Eds.). (2020). *The affect theory reader.* Duke University Press.

Morris, D. (2017). *Merleau-Ponty's developmental ontology.* Northwestern University Press.

O'Mara, S. (2019). *In praise of walking: The new science of how we walk and why it's good for us.* Random House.

Pink, S. (2015). Going forward through the world: Thinking theoretically about first person perspective digital ethnography. *Integrative Psychological and Behavioral Science, 49*(2), 239–252.

Raggatt, P. T. (2000). Mapping the dialogical self: Towards a rationale and method of assessment. *European Journal of Personality, 14*(1), 65–90.

Rousseau, J.-J. (1995). *Reveries of the solitary walker.* Hackett Publishing.

Schön, D. A. (2017). *The reflective practitioner: How professionals think in action.* Routledge.

Shapiro, L., & Stolz, S. (2019). Embodied cognition and its significance for education. *Theory and Research in Education, 17*(1), 19–39.

Shirvani, E., & Shirvani, M. (2023). Absence of embodied subject in the history of philosophy. *Open Journal of Philosophy, 13,* 478–494. https://doi.org/10.4236/ojpp.2023.133032

Snowber, C. (2012). Dancing a curriculum of hope: Cultivating passion as an embodied inquiry. *Journal of Curriculum Theorizing, 28*(2), 118–125. https://journal.jctonline.org/index.php/jct/article/view/369

Snowber, C. (2016). *Embodied inquiry: Writing, living and being through the body.* Springer.

Valsiner, J. (2024). *Dynamic semiosis.* Springer.

van Loon, R. (2024). Exploring the Bodily Self. Generating new meaning through your body – Invited lecture and workshop. Book of Abstracts. In *12th International Conference on the Dialogical Self, June 4–7, 2024, Tallinn, Estonia.*

Zembylas, M. (2007). Emotional ecology: The intersection of emotional knowledge and pedagogical content knowledge in teaching. *Teaching and Teacher Education, 23*(4), 355–367.

CHAPTER 6

INNER SPEAK: DWELLING IN TEACHER PROFESSIONAL DEVELOPMENT

ABSTRACT

Drawing on the Dialogical Self-Theory, this chapter explores the dynamic nature of inner speech through an autoethnographic lens. Through situated narratives from professional life, I examine how these internal voices intersect, conflict, and support meaning-making, emotional regulation. The chapter proposes a typology of three interrelated modes of internal dialogue: rhizomatic, shaped, and encapsulated inner speech. By attending to how teachers speak to themselves, especially in complex or uncertain situations, the chapter invites readers to consider inner speech as a site of reflexivity, resistance, and becoming in teacher education. Ultimately, it offers both a theoretical contribution and a methodological proposition for exploring inner speech in vivo, as it unfolds in the everyday practices of academic and professional life.

Keywords: Inner speech; academic; educational contexts; autoethnography; dialogical self-theory

INTRODUCTION

This is an account about a professional experience: the thoughts, images, and sensations that accompany us as we prepare a lesson, debrief after a difficult parent meeting, or wait for the faculty council to begin.

Teacher Dialogical Self, pages 71–81

doi:10.1108/978-1-80686-957-220261007

My alarm rang early. I didn't sleep well.

When I looked at myself in the bathroom mirror, I saw someone pale and slightly apprehensive. I had every reason to feel nervous. In just over an hour, I would be stepping into a lecture theatre filled with teachers and academics for a symposium about innovation in education.

As I stared into the mirror, I became aware of a familiar inner dialogue beginning to unfold. I was speaking to myself – silently, yet clearly. 'Breathe', I said. 'You've done this before' It felt as though I was both speaker and listener, the reassuring voice rising like a well-worn companion.

Psychologists refer to this as inner speech: the internal dialogue we carry out in silence. Close, we find the private speech, in which the words are audible. If you remind yourself silently, 'Don't forget to collect the homework', or say out loud, 'Okay, let's try that again', you are engaging in inner and private speech, respectively. Both forms serve multiple purposes: they help us plan, regulate emotions, manage classroom interactions, and reflect on our pedagogical decisions. Among adults, inner speech is more prevalent and, for psychologists, particularly compelling because of its central role in thought. It's also notoriously difficult to study (Viacheslav et al., 2023).

Inner speech – variously conceptualised as silent language, verbal thought, or non-vocalised thinking – has long been framed within developmental and cognitive traditions as a mechanism for problem-solving and executive control (Piaget, 1922; Vygotsky, 1934). Yet, emerging scholarship offers a more complex understanding, foregrounding aspects such as its degree of voluntariness, its symbolic and structural properties, and the dynamic interplay between regulated and spontaneous inner dialogue (Cresswell, 2013; Fossa, 2022; Rosenthal, 2012). Advances in research methodologies and a more nuanced understanding of the mind have brought inner speech into sharper focus (Alderson-Day & Fernyhough, 2015; Pacheco & Fossa, 2023): as both a window into teacher cognition and a tool that supports professional agency, resilience, and creativity. Indeed, we are beginning to understand that inner speech doesn't just accompany our day – it shapes how we think, feel, and grow as educators.

The chapter is structured as follows. First, I present the theoretical framework on inner speech. I then introduce a methodological play: rather than framing the chapter as a linear presentation of results or as an argumentative synthesis, I chose to approach it as a performative reflection. This play unfolds through three interrelated modes – rhizomatic, shaped, and encapsulated inner speaking – followed by a practical application to the analysis of professional situations.

THEORETICAL FRAMEWORK: INNER SPEECH

Vygotsky (1934/1987) conceptualised inner speech as the internalized form of social dialogue, emerging through a developmental transition from external speech to private speech and ultimately to silent verbal thought.

According to Vygotsky, all higher psychological functions are first experienced on the social (interpsychological) plane before being internalized at the individual (intrapsychological) level. In this view, inner speech is not merely silent speech, but a qualitatively distinct mode of thought, characterised by condensed syntax, semantic density, and a dialogical structure reflective of its social origins (Vygotsky, 1987). Vygotsky emphasised that inner speech serves a self-regulatory function, enabling individuals to plan, problem-solve, and manage emotional and cognitive processes. Unlike external speech, which is directed towards communication with others, inner speech is oriented towards the self and plays a crucial role in the organisation of conscious thought. This process is particularly evident in early childhood, where private speech – audible self-talk – gradually becomes internalized as children learn to regulate their behaviour independently (Winsler et al., 2009). Recent research inspired by Vygotsky's work has shown that inner speech continues to support adult cognition, particularly in tasks requiring executive function, working memory, and self-monitoring (Alderson-Day & Fernyhough, 2015). These findings reaffirm Vygotsky's claim that language mediates thought and underscore the importance of cultural and interpersonal interaction in the development of inner mental life.

> Inner speech is a special formation in its psychological nature, a special form of verbal activity, with its own characteristics, and which maintains a complex relationship with other forms of verbal activity. We believe that it is not indifferent if one speaks to oneself or others. Internal language is language for oneself and external language is language for others. It cannot be admitted that this radical and fundamental difference between the functions of these kinds of languages has no consequences on the structural nature of both verbal functions... This is not just about vocalisation. The presence or absence of vocalisation does not explain the psychological nature of internal language but the consequence that follows from this nature. Inner speech not only precedes external language, but quite the contrary. External language is the process of transforming thought into word, its materialisation and objectivation. Inner speech is a process in the opposite direction that goes from the outside to the inside, a process of evaporation of language in thought. Vygotsky (1934, pp. 306–307).

Bühler (1934/1965) in his classic works on language and expression revisits an old tradition that is omitted from the study of language and gesture in modern psychology: the theory of human expressiveness. This is observed in ordinary language and in the physiognomic manifestation that accompanies it. Vygotsky did in his work on this phenomenon it is possible to observe in action the Buhlerian expressive dimension. It is in the motivational sphere of consciousness – as the initial stage on which inner speech emerges – that the key to understanding the expressiveness and physiognomy of language exists in the Vygotsky reflections.

The expressive dimension of inner speech is a manifestation of the deeper states of consciousness, that is, the expressiveness of the volitional sphere – motivation that resonates in our interior in the form of a condensed experience of images, thoughts and affections. The subjectivity of conscience is the starting point of human communication and the constructed message its result, thereby constituting the speaking experience – to himself and others – a presentation and not just a representational act (Shanon, 2008).

Fossa (2022) proposes a reconceptualisation of inner speech – not merely as a psychological mechanism tied to problem-solving, but as a private space for remembering, playing, and dreaming (Fossa & Pacheco, 2022; Fossa et al., 2020). Rather than focussing solely on instrumental functions, this perspective emphasises the internal, subjective dimensions of human life. It is in this inner realm that memory, play, and imagination assume a central role – not for the purpose of solving problems, but for revisiting the past, inhabiting a personal and reflective space during moments of leisure or routine, and for envisioning the future, whether near or distant. As Fossa insightfully notes, "in the course of ordinary life, we need to listen to ourselves" (p. 84), highlighting the existential and affective significance of inner speech as a form of self-presence and internal dialogue.

METHODOLOGICAL PLAY

Rather than framing this chapter as a linear presentation of results or an argumentative synthesis, I chose to approach it as a performative reflection, shaped by the very dynamics it explores (Fink, 2016; Impedovo, 2025).

Inspired by the work of Marková (2022) and Fossa (2022) who foreground the spontaneity and multiplicity of inner speech, I allowed the writing itself to become a kind of auto-dialogue – a site where internal voices meet, challenge, and inform each other.

The intention was not to decode or evaluate, but to invite the reader into an active space of listening, imagining, and inner dialogue. I began not with a formal plan, but with a quiet question that emerged somewhere between hesitation and intuition:

> What if I allowed this writing to be a space where I don't just write about inner speech – but write through it, even from within it in a more personal and creative way?

The thought was quickly met by an internal voice – critical, slightly weary, protective of academic norms:

> That sounds bizarre. Can the scholar chapter keep a good academic rigour if written in a non standard way? Are you not expected to maintain an internal coherence and a standard structure?

Then, another voice responded with calm insistence:

> Educators, too, are entitled to a reflective and imaginative space? The writing process is quickly changing, and academic writing will be soon questioned… So better to change!

In that tension, I recognized a familiar inner choreography. The voice of the professional self, shaped by institutional routines, journal guidelines, and calls for objectivity, stood in conversation with the voice of the pedagogical self – the one that listens, experiments, and allows emotion and body to enter the frame of knowledge-making.

> One morning, as I sat down to write, I was distracted by noise from the street below: machinery, voices, footsteps. A minor irritation surfaced, narrating itself in real-time: "You'll never be able to write like this – close the window, block the sound." Another voice intervened, more resigned than helpful: "It's not worth fighting. Maybe today's not a writing day." But then, a third voice emerged, quieter but more grounded: "The noise is here. The challenge is not full silence, but to advance in the chapter.

In that moment, I recognized how external disruptions mirrored internal ones due to the pressure to meet the deadlines, and how writing activity could become a practice of negotiation rather than mastery. Starting the process of writing the chapter and taking notes of the ongoing inner speech, I noticed the shifting of attention towards lived experience – towards sensation, pause, rhythm, and the unspoken aspects of reflection. I noticed how nuanced voices emerged as meta positions between contrasting voices, sometimes to hold paradox and to conciliate positions.

This chapter, therefore, is not only about inner speech in theory – it is also an attempt to perform the conditions under which it becomes knowable.

A DIALOGICAL ENTRY INTO WRITING: IDENTIFY THREE MODALITIES

In reflecting on my own inner speech throughout the writing of this chapter, I began to recognise the plurality of forms and functions that it can take. Rather than being a stable or unified phenomenon, inner speech appears – at least in my experience – as a dynamic, shifting, and stratified landscape, shaped by emotion, context, and intention. Drawing on the model of spontaneous thought (Andrews-Hanna et al., 2017), I propose a heuristic distinction among three interrelated modes: rhizomatic, shaped, and encapsulated inner speaking.

Rhizomatic Inner Speaking

This mode of inner speech is non-linear, fragmented, and associative. It resists control and proliferates across mental domains – emotions, memories, sensations, concepts – without predetermined logic. Inspired by Deleuze and Guattari's (1987) metaphor of the rhizome, this form of inner dialogue is fertile and generative, yet often chaotic. It mirrors the default mode network in neuroscience, activated during mind-wandering and unstructured thought (Smallwood & Schooler, 2015).

In my case, rhizomatic inner speech tends to emerge when I overthink a problem, particularly under pressure. Rather than resolving the issue, this over-analysis multiplies interpretations, creates doubt, and disrupts decision-making.

> Should I rephrase this again? What if the literature I'm referencing is outdated? Why haven't I looked at X's framework yet? Maybe this whole section should be cut...

This excess of internal branching, while intellectually rich, often paralyses action. I have come to realize that letting go of the need to interpret everything is itself an intelligent act. As I wrote in my notes:

> Over-analysing keeps me down – this has been my experience these last few days. Sometimes the most generative move is to stop decoding and start acting.

Shaped Inner Speaking

In contrast, shaped inner speech emerges when I begin to give form to thought – not by suppressing spontaneity, but by orienting it towards a meaningful goal. This is the kind of inner talk that mediates between reflection and action, integrating insights and channelling them into coherent expression. It echoes what Vygotsky (1934/1987) described as the transformation of external speech into internalized, goal-directed thought.

During the writing of this chapter, I experienced shaped inner speech most clearly when I accepted that understanding is a process, not a prerequisite. I was new to the empirical literature on inner speech, particularly in its biological and neuroscientific dimensions. The conceptual load triggered doubts about adequacy, fluency, and epistemic legitimacy.

> Am I competent enough to write about this?
>
> There is so much I haven't read...
>
> Focus on what you understand today. You can always revise later.

This internal negotiation helped me regain agency. By acknowledging the limits of my current understanding without diminishing its value, I was able to continue. Shaped inner speaking thus functions as an internal scaffolding that helps regulate effort and sustain commitment.

Encapsulated Inner Speaking

The third mode I observed is encapsulated inner speech, a form of dialogical contraction. It tends to appear in emotionally charged or high-stakes situations, when the self retreats into a directive, condensed, and often bilingual command. It feels like a narrowing of the dialogical space – less open-ended than the other two modes, but sometimes instrumental in breaking inertia.

> Now do it. Write. Don't waste time. Focus.

In these moments, the inner dialogue does not explore or inquire. It is a discipline. This voice is sometimes authoritarian, sometimes maternal, always urgent. It reminds me that I am located in a specific social and professional context, where time, responsibility, and performance are not abstractions but immediate demands. And yet, even in its rigidity, encapsulated inner speech holds a form of care – it protects momentum, it insists on moving forward.

Extended Application: Analysis of a Professional Situations

These distinctions – rhizomatic, shaped, and encapsulated inner speaking – are not intended as heuristic tools for deepening our understanding of inner speech in daily academic and educational life. Within the context of teacher education, recognising these internal movements enables the cultivation of metacognitive awareness, emotional self-regulation, and professional self-authorship.

In practice, these forms of inner speech rarely occur in isolation. They overlap, interrupt, and inform one another, often within a single interaction or moment of decision-making. The following lived episode exemplifies how the three modes dynamically coexisted in the span of a few minutes – a meeting with a school principal regarding professional development leave. It highlights the embodied, emotional, and strategic layers of inner speech, particularly as experienced by educators negotiating institutional contexts.

> Upon arriving at the office of the school principal, I noticed that another administrative colleague had entered the room uninvited, seeking to speak with him. I observed a faint irritation within myself – an inner stirring – but resolved not to be discouraged.

At that very moment, multiple inner scenes opened up simultaneously. The upcoming three-day professional development course I had applied for felt significant; I hoped to be granted approval. Yet the circumstances of the meeting shifted quickly: the principal exited the room, acknowledged our appointment briefly, then returned and became visibly agitated by a phone call he had just received.

Here, my rhizomatic inner speech activated.

> He's distracted now… Maybe he won't really listen. What if this isn't the right time? Should I try again next week? Maybe he'll forget… But if I don't speak now, the deadline will pass… And that colleague – why did she come in right now?

Thoughts and associations branched out in every direction – non-linear, emotionally charged, anticipatory, and largely out of my control. The noise, unpredictability, and emotional climate of the situation echoed earlier theoretical descriptions of spontaneous thought and mental time travel (Andrews-Hanna et al., 2017), pulling me into imagined futures and past frustrations.

At the same time, a shaped inner voice intervened, grounding me:

> Stay calm. Wait patiently. Don't show frustration. When it's your turn, be clear and focused. You're here with a purpose.

This regulative voice, shaped through years of professional interaction, helped stabilise my attention. It invited me to inhabit the situation with intention and containment, rather than reaction. It reflected an internalized dialogical practice cultivated through experience: not the repression of emotion, but its attunement and redirection towards meaningful agency.

Then, the moment of action arrived. The principal asked, gently, if we could speak in the corridor, due to the crowded conditions of his office. I accepted calmly and, once there, spoke directly:

> It's very important to me to attend this professional development course.

I explained my motivations, reminded him there were no conflicting responsibilities during those dates, and expressed my trust in the process. At this point, encapsulated inner speech emerged - a compressed, imperative voice that pushed me forward with clarity:

> Now go. Say it. Don't waste time. Focus.

Unlike the earlier rhizomatic wandering or the shaped inner guidance, this mode of inner speech was directive, urgent, and affectively sharp – a compact force of self-mobilisation, typical in high-stakes professional moments. It is not dialogical in the exploratory sense but dialogical in its forceful attempt to cut through internal noise and anchor action in the immediate present.

Eventually, the principal paused, looked at me, and replied:

> Remind me of the dates later on, and we'll figure out how to submit the request, what motivation to include…

A resolution, modest but meaningful, was reached. Not just because of external permission, but because of an internal negotiation that had taken place in the background – a dialogue between voices, each necessary, each partial, each shaping the self-in-action.

Episodes like this are not exceptional in educators' lives – they are ordinary moments charged with ethical and relational complexity (Impedovo, 2021). By examining such micro-interactions through the lens of inner speech, teacher educators and researchers alike can better understand how thought is lived, embodied, and entangled with institutional and affective ecologies.

Engaging pre-service and in-service teachers in recognising these modes – by writing them, voicing them, and reflecting on them – can help them develop tools for resilience, clarity, and dialogical presence. It is not only what we say in these moments that matters, but how we speak to ourselves in the interstices of tension and possibility.

CONCLUSION

This chapter, conceived as a performative act of writing, reflects the central question I wish to contribute to the broader conversation of this volume: What if we explored ways to inquire into inner speech publicly – not merely as a retrospective phenomenon captured through reflective interviews, but as a living, dynamic presence within pedagogical and academic interactions? Could we begin to engage with inner speech in real time – as it happens – within the spaces of our conferences, our classrooms, and the written dialogs of academic journals?

In composing this chapter, I chose to inhabit the reflective and imaginative spirit of the topic. At the conclusion of the process, in the quiet aftermath of such a dialogical episode, an inspiration for the composition of haiku emerged. Haiku[1] is a type of short form poetry that originated in Japan. Traditional Japanese haiku consists of three phrases composed of 17 morae in a 5, 7, 5 pattern. It emerged to encapsulate the essence of inner speech as lived experience – where tension becomes rhythm, and thought becomes breath:

> Inner voices stir,
>
> morning noise meets thought's silence –
>
> words begin to breathe.

It is both a poetic and pedagogical reminder that the voice within is never singular, but always relational, situated, and in motion.

As a teacher educator, I allowed myself to write with the same openness I wish to find more often: to play with language, to follow affective traces, and to attend to the shifting identity positions that shape our professional becoming. This goes along with my desire to trouble the boundaries between scholarship and lived experience. Through this chapter, I hoped to momentarily step outside the scripted routines of academic discourse – while still engaging them critically and from within. In doing so, I was looking to give a contribution that is both situated in and reflective of our professional practices as educators: practices where inner speech is not only methodological concerns but a lived experience.

NOTE

1. https://en.wikipedia.org/wiki/Haiku.

REFERENCES

Alderson-Day, B., & Fernyhough, C. (2015). Inner speech: Development, cognitive functions, phenomenology, and neurobiology. *Psychological Bulletin, 141*(5), 931–965. https://doi.org/10.1037/bul0000021

Bühler, K. (1965). *Theory of language: The representational function of language.* John Benjamins Publishing Company.

Cresswell, J. (2013). *Qualitative inquiry & research design: Choosing among five approaches.* Sage.

Deleuze, G., & Guattari, F. (1987). *A thousand plateaus: Capitalism and schizophrenia.* University of Minnesota Press.

Fink, E. (2016). *Play as symbol of the world and other writings.* Indiana University Press.

Fossa, P. (Ed.). (2022). *New perspectives on inner speech.* Springer.

Fossa, P., & Pacheco, C. (2022). Reflective and pre-reflective inner speech. In P. Fossa (Ed.), *New perspectives on inner speech* (pp. 9–21). Springer International Publishing. https://doi.org/10.1007/978-3-031-06847-8_2

Fossa, P., Pérez, R. M., & Marcotti, C. M. (2020). The relationship between the inner speech and emotions: Revisiting the study of passions in psychology. *Human Arenas, 3*(2), 229–246.

Impedovo, M. A. (2021). *Identity and teacher professional development: A reflective, collaborative and agentive learning journey.* SPRINGER BRIEF. ISBN 978-3-030-71367-6. https://link.springer.com/book/10.1007/978-3-030-71367-6

Impedovo, M. (2025). Mirroring the self through Hamlet affective aesthetic experience. *Integrative Psychological and Behavioral Science, 59*(3), 1–16.

Marková, I. (2022). Enacting inner speech on the academic stage. A dialogical review. In P. Fossa, (Ed.), *New perspectives on inner speech.* Springer.

Pacheco, C., & Fossa, P. (2023). An inner forest of experiences and possibilities: Creativity and imagination from a pre-reflective perspective. *Human Arenas,* 1–17.

Piaget, J. (1922). Essai sur la multiplication logique et les débuts de la pensée formelle chez l'enfant.

Rosenthal, V. (2012). La voix de l'intérieur. *Intellectica, 58*(2), 53–89.
Shanon, B. (2008). A psychological theory of consciousness. *Journal of Consciousness Studies, 15*(5), 5–47.
Smallwood, J., & Schooler, J. W. (2015). The science of mind wandering empirically navigating the stream of consciousness. *Annual Review of Psychology, 3*(66), 487–518. https://doi.org/10.1146/annurev-psych-010814-015331
Viacheslav, I., Vartanov, A., Bueva, A., & Bronov, O. (2023). The emotional component of inner speech: A pilot exploratory fMRI study. *Brain and Cognition, 165*, 105939.
Vygotsky, L. S. (1987). Thinking and speech (N. Minick, Trans.). In R. W. Rieber & A. S. Carton (Eds.), *The collected works of L. S. Vygotsky: Vol. 1. Problems of general psychology* (pp. 39–285). Plenum Press.
Vygotsky, L. S. (1934/1986). *Thought and language.* The MIT Press.
Winsler, A., Fernyhough, C., & Montero, I. (2009). *Private speech, executive functioning, and the development of verbal self-regulation.* Cambridge University Press.

CHAPTER 7

THE MUTUAL FEEDING OF ACTION AND REFLECTION AS A DIALOGICAL PROCESS

ABSTRACT

This chapter explores the mutual feeding of action and reflection in academic life through an autoethnographic approach. Drawing on Dialogical Self Theory, I examine the inner speech between multiple 'I-positions' that animate teacher professional practice. Through the evocation of distinct inner voices – each rooted in lived experience and institutional positioning – I investigate how internal dialogs contribute to decision-making, identity negotiation, and research orientation. Writing from within the fields of academic life, this chapter offers a performative inquiry into the tensions, contradictions, and generative forces that shape scholarly becoming.

Keywords: Teacher educator; autoethnographic; inner speech; dialogical self theory; inquiry

INTRODUCTION

This chapter emerges from a broader inquiry: What are the 'I-positions' that constitute my current academic life? How do these positions speak, clash, and collaborate in shaping my research and teaching? Using an auto-dialogic method, I reflect on how these inner positions become interlocutors in my professional development, enabling what Vygotsky (1987) called

Teacher Dialogical Self, pages 83–92

doi:10.1108/978-1-80686-957-220261008

the 'internalisation of social dialogue' and what Hermans (2001) frames as the dynamic self-inhabiting a multivoiced space.

Dialogical Self Theory (Hermans & Kempen, 1993) posits the self as composed of multiple I-positions, each with a voice, perspective, and narrative tone. These positions may reflect roles (e.g., 'I as researcher'), affective states ('I as exhausted', 'I as hopeful'), or institutional identities. Rather than seeing these as dissonant distractions, the dialogical approach recognises them as constitutive of thought and self-understanding.

This study aligns with autoethnographic methods (Ellis et al., 2011), where personal narrative becomes a lens to examine broader cultural and institutional structures. Here, the auto-dialogue becomes both data and method – a performative exploration of the tensions and coherences that animate the inner life of academic work. This approach offers not only a method for self-understanding but also a pedagogical practice for those who teach, mentor, and research in complex, relational settings.

The chapter is structured as follows. The theoretical framework is grounded in the mutual interplay of action and reflection. To investigate this interplay in professional practice, the study adopts an auto-dialogue methodology. A specific situation is presented as the focal example for application. From this, the process is articulated in three steps: identifying the position, naming the position, and expressing and sharing it.

The Mutual Feeding of Action and Reflection as a Dialogical Process

In the evolving landscape of professional and educational inquiry, the relationship between action and reflection has been widely acknowledged as a cornerstone of learning and development. However, rather than conceptualising this relationship as a linear alternation – acting, then reflecting – this chapter proposes to understand the mutual feeding of action and reflection as a dialogical process. Such a framing suggests not only that action gives rise to reflection and vice versa, but that both are co-constituted through inner and outer dialogs (Fossa et al., 2019), deeply situated in cultural, relational, and temporal contexts.

Traditional models of professional development, such as Schön's (1983) notion of reflection-in-action and reflection-on-action, emphasise the temporal and cognitive distinction between the moment of doing and the subsequent moment of thinking about doing. While these models have advanced our understanding of practitioner knowledge, they often preserve a dichotomy between practice and thought, suggesting that reflection occurs retrospectively, external to the immediacy of experience.

A dialogical perspective complicates this sequence. Drawing on Bakhtin's (1981) philosophy of language and Hermans' (2001) Dialogical Self Theory, reflection is not a solitary mental operation, but a polyphonic process – a conversation among multiple 'I-positions' within the self and across time, space, and social others. In this view, action and reflection are not separate phases, but intertwined moments in an ongoing internal and external dialogue.

Vygotsky's (1934/1987) theory of inner speech deepens this understanding by locating reflective consciousness within a developmental, mediated, and social framework. For Vygotsky, inner speech emerges through the internalisation of social interaction and becomes a psychological tool for self-regulation, problem-solving, and meaning making. When a professional or educator engages in reflection, they are not merely recalling or analysing events; they are speaking with themselves, replaying dialogs, evaluating actions, rehearsing alternatives, and imagining future possibilities. This internal dialogue is not limited to rational analysis. It is shaped by emotion, memory, embodiment, and voice. Often, a practitioner's inner speech carries the residue of institutional norms, student voices, past mentors, or conflicting identities. The reflective process, in this sense, is not only cognitive but dialogical – a space where action and interpretation meet, collide, and co-evolve.

Conversely, action itself is dialogical. Every pedagogical or professional act is already embedded in responsive contexts – framed by previous decisions, shaped by the presence of others, and oriented towards anticipated responses. As Bakhtin (1981) reminds us, every utterance is a response to previous utterances and anticipates future ones. Similarly, every professional action is a response – to a situation, a value, a memory, or an imagined outcome.

This means that even while acting, professionals are reflecting-in-the-moment, negotiating meaning, adjusting strategies, and responding to inner and outer feedback. In other words, action is never mute – it is already saturated with responsive awareness.

When action and reflection are viewed as mutually feeding through dialogical movement, professional practice becomes a form of living inquiry (Marshall, 1999). Rather than isolating reflection as a separate activity, professionals can be seen as constantly inhabiting a space of negotiation – between intention and uncertainty, between multiple voices, and between the known and the emergent.

This dialogical view also invites an ethic of reflexive humility. Practitioners and researchers alike are not the sole authors of their actions or insights. Instead, they become participants in a multi-voiced, context-sensitive conversation that unfolds over time. The professional self becomes not a fixed identity but a relational position, always in the process of being re-authored through the interplay of action and reflection.

METHODOLOGICAL APPROACH

To explore the dialogical interplay between action and reflection in professional practice, this study adopts an auto-dialogue methodology. Rooted in autoethnography (Ellis et al., 2011) and Dialogical Self Theory (Hermans, 2001), this approach invites the researcher to engage in a structured and reflexive dialogue with their own inner voices, positioning the self not as a unified entity but as a multivoiced subject in constant negotiation with lived experiences.

The choice of auto-dialogue as a method is grounded in the belief that inner speech, often overlooked in formal research, is a rich source of data on professional identity, decision-making, and emotional labour (Fossa, 2017). For teachers, the internal conversations we conduct with ourselves – before, during, and after pedagogical actions – are not merely anecdotal or psychological by-products. They are central to how we construct meaning, justify choices, and sustain engagement in complex educational environments.

Auto-dialogue offers a means of making this invisible labour audible, tracing the subtle movements of thought that accompany, disrupt, or support action.

Specifically, to investigate the dialogical dynamics of the self within my academic practice, I engaged in a structured self-reflective exercise inspired by the notion of I-positions. The process unfolded in three interconnected phases:

- Identification of I-Positions: The first phase involves identifying the various I-positions currently active in one's academic or professional life. These may include institutional roles (e.g., I as teacher, I as researcher, I as administrator), personal roles (I as parent, I as learner), or affective/ethical positions (I as hopeful, I as overwhelmed, I as critic). I began by mapping the diverse roles, perspectives, and emotional orientations currently active in my academic life – for example, the teacher, the researcher, the mentor, the colleague. Each position was acknowledged as a distinct voice within the self, carrying its own priorities, concerns, and affective tone.
- Voicing and Articulation: Once identified, each I-position was invited to 'speak' in the first person, producing short utterances that reflected its perspective (e.g., 'As a teacher, I feel exhausted by certain classroom dynamics'). These statements were not polished narratives but rather fragments of thought, affect, and attitude. The writing may take the form of first-person monologs, inner dialogs, letters to the self, or stream-of-consciousness accounts. They were read aloud – or silently – allowing for a more embodied

engagement with the different tonalities and intensities of each voice. These utterances are not fictional; they emerge from attending to inner speech, often in moments of decision-making, fatigue, or inspiration.

- Dialogical Reflection: Finally, I attended to the interplay among these voices, noting moments of convergence, contradiction, and negotiation. Once voices are externalised, the researcher reads them aloud (or silently), noticing interactions among them. Some voices dominate; others remain in the margins. Some conflict directly; others echo, affirm, or interrupt. This step involved reflecting on how such inner dialogs shape my current research questions, methodological choices, and broader professional stance. *Which voices feel legitimate? Which are silenced? What institutional or cultural norms are these voices speaking through? What tensions, values, or aspirations emerge in the dialogue?* This step opens space for ethical, emotional, and epistemological reflection on the internal politics of the self. The analysis privileged the emergent quality of the dialogue, considering not only what each voice said, but how their interaction generated new insights or tensions relevant to my academic trajectory. Through this method, inner speech was approached not as a static cognitive phenomenon, but as a living dialogical process – one that mediates action, reflection, and the ongoing construction of professional identity.
- Reintegrating Insights into Professional Contexts: The final phase involves reintegrating insights into the researcher's broader professional or educational context. Rather than treating the auto-dialogue as a private catharsis, it becomes a method of inquiry – a way of generating theoretical insight and pedagogical responsiveness. This reintegration may take several forms: Analytical memos in a research project; Reflective writing for publication; Dialogue with colleagues or students; Transformation of professional routines or choices.

Findings: The Voices Within

These voices do not coexist peacefully. Some compete, others whisper. The teacher-educator and the researcher often negotiate time and attention. The administrator imposes order while the mother resists being scheduled. Yet their dialogue reveals not fragmentation but depth – a textured account of the academic self as layered, ethical, and evolving. The act of listening to these voices became a moment of what Schön

(1983) calls reflection-in-action. The inner speech I captured was not retrospective; it was immediate, embodied, and shaping my choices in real time. The mutual feeding of action and reflection is not a solitary act but a conversation among selves. In writing this chapter, I did not resolve my tensions. I inhabited them. I listened. I asked: What would it mean to write not from a single 'I' but from a chorus of selves, each bearing wisdom, fatigue, and desire? Through dialogical self-inquiry, we might reimagine academic identity not as a stable form but as a living negotiation, a reflective performance grounded in voice, vulnerability, and relational thought.

In this quiet morning of writing, I became aware not of silence, but of noise – both external and internal. The external came from a chainsaw, slicing through my concentration. The internal came from voices: one annoyed, another lazy, yet another anxious about deadlines. Amidst this polyphony, I paused – not to control or silence – but to listen. What I encountered was not merely distraction, but a dialogical self at work: an academic self-fragmented, shifting, alive in its multiplicity. The 'Teacher' voice says: 'I'm tired of always performing with certainty. I want to admit I don't know. That I'm learning too. Sometimes I feel emptied before I start.'

The 'Researcher' voice replies: 'But uncertainty doesn't get funded. We need to stay relevant and publishable. Still, I believe in this inquiry – it's worth the effort.' I as Administrator: 'Too many forms, too many meetings. I feel distant from the pedagogical heart of my work.' I as Student-of-the-Field: 'I want to stay curious. But I fear irrelevance. Am I still learning or just producing?'

Auto-dialogue as method necessitates attentiveness to vulnerability, exposure, and interpretation. The researcher is invited to navigate the ethics of voicing private thought in public space and remain critically aware of the partiality and constructed nature of all internal narratives. As a methodological stance, auto-dialogue resists closure and embraces complexity. It foregrounds reflection not as a discrete phase but as an ongoing dialogical movement entangled with action. By listening to our own inner speech, we begin to map the landscape of our professional becoming – a terrain shaped as much by conflicting voices as by coherent plans. In this way, auto-dialogue becomes a method not just for self-study, but for deep engagement with the multiplicity of the educator's self.

Moving Professional I-Positions

Teaching often invites us to navigate moments of tension between acting and holding back. These moments, though seemingly ordinary, reveal the complex choreography of inner dialogs that accompany professional practice. One such instance occurred during a lab session with my students, who had been instructed – both verbally and in writing on the board – to carry out a task autonomously.

> *There was a part of me that wanted to react, and another part that told me to wait. One example comes from working with my students. They were assigned a lab task to design an activity. After giving the instructions, I told them – verbally and in writing on the board – that they needed to do the activity independently and not keep asking for clarification. Still, they were anxious and continued to ask questions repeatedly. I had clearly written on the board that they had to do it alone. A part of me wanted to answer their questions and guide them through the task – just to move things forward, especially since time was passing. But another part said, 'Wait. Observe.'*
>
> *So, I saw this as an opportunity: 'Alright, this is my chance.' Even if it wasn't perfect, I decided to hold the line. It wasn't easy. And then it happened again in the next class – with older children. I expected them to carry out the task with more autonomy.*

Despite the (my supposed) clarity of my guidance, their uncertainty surfaced quickly. They began asking repeated questions, clearly seeking reassurance. Part of me was inclined to respond – eager to clarify, to guide, and to preserve the pace of the lesson. Time was slipping by, and the pressure to move forward was real. But simultaneously, another voice within urged restraint: 'Wait. Observe.' In that pause, a space opened – not just for the students, but for me. I recognized the moment as an opportunity to trust the process, to uphold the value of learner autonomy, even if the outcome might not be seamless. Later that day, a similar scenario unfolded in a class with older students. My expectations for greater independence were again confronted by questions, hesitation, and the pull to step in. Once more, I experienced the tension between the impulse to act and the reflective choice to wait.

What these episodes demonstrate is not simply a pedagogical strategy, but a deeper process: the mutual feeding of action and reflection as an internal, dialogical negotiation (Morioka, 2015). We can understand these moments as the interplay of multiple I-positions – voices within the self that speak from different priorities, emotions, and professional identities. One voice may prioritise efficiency, another autonomy; one may express anxiety, another trust. Their interaction does not follow a linear logic of 'act first, reflect later,' but rather unfolds as a simultaneous internal dialogue, shaping decisions in real time.

The concept of reflection-in-action (Schön, 1983) is particularly resonant here. Reflection does not merely happen after the fact – it is embedded within the moment of hesitation, the decision to withhold, the subtle shift from instruction to observation. In that liminal space, uncertainty becomes a pedagogical terrain rather than a threat.

These recursive experiences across contexts reveal an important truth: teacher professionalism is not just a matter of competence or decision-making, but of ethical self-inquiry. Each action – or deliberate non-action – raises the question: Who am I being, and who am I becoming, in this moment as an educator?

Such questioning does not seek definitive answers. Rather, it acknowledges that teaching is a relational, situated, and evolving practice. Like rhizomatic growth, reflection branches laterally, not hierarchically feeding back into future moments of choice. The oscillation between knowing and not knowing, asserting and withholding, speaking and listening is not a failure of consistency, but a mark of attunement.

From the Situation to General Guidance

To give shape to this process, three directions are proposed – also elaborated in Impedovo (2026) to analyse the academic working-class identity.

Pointing the Position, Naming the Position, and Expressing and Sharing – serve as guidance for understanding and navigating the complexities of self-identity in relation to others. Here's how each dimension:

Pointing the Position: Reflecting on personal past from the current perspective to identify how the identity position clearly manifests in one's identity. Example: Reflecting on how my working-class experience influences the perception of current academic practices. Facilitates the integration of past experiences into the current self-concept, which is vital for coherent self-narrative construction.

Naming the Position: Characterising the identity position by contextualising it within broader perspectives or other viewpoints. Example: Analysing the identity position as a convergence between working-class identity and academic expectations, considering social and cultural structures. By naming their identity positions, individuals can better understand how these positions align or conflict with societal roles and norms. This process involves recognising how one's personal experiences and perspectives intersect with broader societal frameworks. This dimension aids in understanding how identity is constructed and influenced by external social and cultural factors, enhancing awareness of how different voices and positions interact with societal expectations.

Expressing and sharing: Communicating and sharing the identity position with others, highlighting the implications for practice and theory. Example: Sharing personal experiences of discomfort in academic settings with colleagues and students to promote better understanding and inclusive practices. Expressing and sharing allows individuals to voice their experiences and perspectives, contributing to the representation of diverse identities in social interactions. It supports the negotiation of self-concept in response to others' feedback and perspectives. Promotes the articulation of personal identity positions in social contexts, enhancing dialogue between self and others.

Together, these dimensions support a comprehensive understanding of the self as a dynamic and dialogical construct, continuously negotiated through internal and external interactions.

Understanding reflection and action as dialogically interwoven has implications for how we train educators, design curricula, and conduct practitioner research. It encourages:

- Valuing inner speech and self-talk as legitimate sites of inquiry.
- Creating pedagogical spaces for multiple voices to be heard and reflected upon.
- Using writing, dialogue, and narrative as tools not just for representation but for thinking-in-practice.
- Embracing inquiry as a way of being, not only as a research method.

In teacher education, this approach suggests moving beyond decontextualised models of competence towards more narrative, embodied, and situated practices of professional learning. It affirms that knowledge emerges not only from analysis but from attentiveness to the dialogs we carry within and around us, and from the courage to pause, speak, and listen – to ourselves, to others, and to the unfinishedness of our own becoming.

CONCLUSION

This analysis has shown how the self, especially in academic and professional life, is not singular but dialogical, composed of multiple positions that speak, overlap, and sometimes compete. By pointing, naming, and expressing these I-positions, we create a space for reflexive insight and ethical engagement. The work is not to choose one voice over another, but to stay with the conversation, learning to listen more deeply – to ourselves, to others, and to the contradictions that make us human.

REFERENCES

Bakhtin, M. M. (1981). *The dialogic imagination: Four essays* (M. Holquist, Ed.; C. Emerson & M. Holquist, Trans.). University of Texas Press.

Ellis, C., Adams, T. E., & Bochner, A. P. (2011). Autoethnography: An overview. *Forum for Qualitative Social Research, 12*(1). Art. 10. https://doi.org/10.17169/fqs-12.1.1589

Fossa, P., Gonzalez, N., & Cordero Di Montezemolo, F. (2019). From inner speech to mind-wandering: Developing a comprehensive model of inner mental activity trajectories. *Integrative Psychological and Behavioral Science, 53*, 298–322.

Fossa, P. (2017). The expressive dimension of inner speech. *Psicologia USP, 28*, 318–326.

Hermans, H. J. M., & Kempen, H. J. G. (1993). *The dialogical self: Meaning as movement.* Academic Press.

Hermans, H. J. M. (2001). The dialogical self: Toward a theory of personal and cultural positioning. *Culture & Psychology, 7*(3), 243–281. https://doi.org/10.1177/1354067X0173001

Impedovo, M. (2026). De la Classe Ouvrière à l'Académie : Une Perspective Dialogique et Auto-ethnographique sur l'Identité et l'Enseignement. In E. F. Von Fircks (Ed.), *La psychologie culturelle : Des contextes francophones.* Information Age Publishing (IAP) dans la Série Advances in Cultural Psychology (Jaan Valsiner as Series Editor).

Marshall, J. (1999). Living life as inquiry. *Systemic Practice and Action Research, 12*(2), 155–171. https://doi.org/10.1023/A:1022421929640

Morioka, M. (2015). How to create Ma–the living pause–in the landscape of the mind: The wisdom of Nohtheatre. *International Journal for Dialogical Science, 9*(1), 81–95.

Schön, D. A. (1983). *The reflective practitioner: How professionals think in action.* Basic Books.

Vygotsky, L. S. (1987). Thinking and speech. (N. Minick, Trans.). In R. W. Rieber & A. S. Carton (Eds.), *The collected works of L. S. Vygotsky: Vol. 1. Problems of general psychology* (pp. 39–285). Plenum Press.

CHAPTER 8

EMOTION AND TEACHER IDENTITY

ABSTRACT

This chapter explores the role of emotions in the professional life of teachers. Moments of discomfort, tensions and judgements illustrate how teachers and teacher-educators navigate the emotional labyrinth of their work. A metaphor inspired by the myth of Theseus and Ariadne's red thread is employed to frame negative emotions as both obstacles and potential guides: while such emotions can entrap teachers in repetitive cycles of disconnection, reflectivity functions as a 'thread' enabling re-engagement with professional purpose and relational vitality. By interpreting teachers' anecdotes through these Dialogical Self Theory, it becomes clear that negative emotions, when acknowledged and navigated with care, can serve as catalysts for growth, deeper connection, and renewed meaning in the teaching profession.

Keywords: Professional reflection; tension; disconnection; reflectivity; professional growth

INTRODUCTION

In an ongoing discussion about neoliberalism in higher education – expressed in the marketisation of universities and the commodification of education, where students are deemed as customers and academics are evaluated on performance-based metrics (Cannella & Koro-Ljungberg, 2017; del Cerro Santamaria, 2020; Giroux, 2014), it is important to remind

Teacher Dialogical Self, pages 93–102

doi:10.1108/978-1-80686-957-220261009

that teaching is an ongoing professional practice that engages in a communal and cultural process of learning, sensing, and interacting in embodied and relational ways. At its core, teaching unfolds in shared spaces where meanings are co-constructed, negotiated, and at times contested. This process is deeply intertwined with emotional life: the daily interactions between teachers, students, and colleagues inevitably evoke a wide spectrum of emotions – both positive and negative – that shape professional identity and practice (de Kadt & Jawitz, 2018).

Studies show that academics in higher education increasingly encounter emotional strain, often feeling disconnected, undervalued, and overwhelmed by growing pressures linked to accountability and performance indicators (Shahjahan, 2020). The rise of neoliberal managerial practices in universities, with their focus on publications, metrics, and student satisfaction, has intensified insecurity and negatively affected mental health (Maisuria & Helmes, 2019). In addition, academics are required to manage their own emotional challenges while simultaneously addressing students' expectations and wellbeing, which further adds to their emotional workload (Nixon & Scullion, 2022).

Emotions are integral to the work of teaching. Managing them effectively requires the development of professional competencies that extend beyond content knowledge and pedagogical skills, encompassing emotional awareness, regulation, and constructive transformation. In this sense, teacher professional development is not only about acquiring strategies and methods, but also about cultivating the capacity to navigate affective complexity within the cultural, historical, and material contexts in which education takes place.

Ferrare and Hora (2014) remind us that meaningful change in educational settings is made possible through a careful cultivation of practice – one that is responsive to the lived, embodied realities of teaching and learning. This involves a sustained commitment to sensing the emotional climate and responding with both professional intentionality and human openness. When approached in this way, teaching becomes a practice of resonance – requiring sensitivity to the rhythms of interaction, the courage to remain open to others, and the ability to transform even moments of negativity into opportunities for connection and growth (do Mar Pereira, 2016).

The chapter is structured as follows. It begins with a discussion of professional teacher identity and Dialogical Self Theory (DST) and the role of emotions. A metaphorical parallel is then drawn between the 'Red Thread of Theseus' and the experience of negative emotions in teaching. This is followed by an analysis of several short narrative teachers' accounts. The chapter concludes with a discussion framing the figure of the teacher through the lens of struggle.

DIALOGICAL SELF THEORY AND EMOTIONS

The notion of professional teacher identity refers to how teachers understand both their practice and themselves as they participate in it (Beauchamp, 2015). Identity can be seen as a mediating resource that shapes an individual's interactions with others, their environment, and their own psychological processes. From this perspective, identity functions as a cultural construct that organizes and connects experiences, allowing individuals and those around them to make sense of and give coherence to actions (Rosa & Valsiner, 2018; Roth & Erstad, 2016). This view of identity highlights how teachers construct meanings through their everyday professional practices, while also underlining the agency they enact within those practices. Such experiences may be understood as conscious constructions of objective situations, emerging from the tension between the characteristics of those situations and individuals' sensory capacities, attentional resources, personal histories, and self-positioning within their life course (Vassilieva & Zavershneva, 2020). Identity should therefore be understood not as a fixed attribute, but as a dynamic and evolving 'technology of the self' (Falsafi & Coll, 2011), emerging within and through participation in socio-cultural practices across the lifespan. In this way, identity and socio-cultural practices are mutually constitutive: as practices shape identity, the transformations of identity, in turn, contribute to reshaping those practices.

Focus on identity, this chapter adopts the theoretical framework of Dialogical Self Theory (DST) (Hermans, 2013). This conceptualises the self as a dynamic multiplicity of 'I-positions' in an imagined landscape of the mind. Each I-position represents a distinct perspective from which the self can speak, act, and feel – such as 'I as a caring teacher', 'I as a frustrated colleague', or 'I as a confident professional'. These positions can be internal (voices within the self) or external (voices of significant others, institutions, or cultural norms that are internalized) (Hermans & Hermans-Konopka, 2010). Emotions in DST are not passive states but dialogical signals: they emerge within and between I-positions, often reflecting the degree of harmony, tension, or conflict in the self's internal dialogue. From this perspective, emotional experiences – especially negative ones – are opportunities for repositioning: by recognising the voices involved and facilitating dialogue between them, the self can achieve greater integration and flexibility. Thus, managing emotions in teaching is not simply a matter of suppression or control, but of fostering constructive inner dialogs that enable the self to respond rather than react. In professional contexts, DST invites teachers to consider emotional episodes as moments of inner negotiation, where affect becomes a catalyst for self-reflection, perspective-taking, and ultimately, professional growth.

In the following section, a metaphorical parallel is then drawn between the 'Red Thread of Theseus' and the experience of negative emotions in teaching.

THE RED THREAD OF THESEUS AND NEGATIVE EMOTIONS IN TEACHING

In the Greek myth of Theseus,[1] the red thread given by Ariadne is the lifeline that allows him to navigate the labyrinth, confront the Minotaur, and, crucially, find his way back out. Without the thread, victory over the Minotaur would have been hollow – Theseus would have remained lost in the darkness, unable to return to the world outside.

In the professional life of a teacher, negative emotions – frustration, disappointment, resentment – can feel like a labyrinth. Daily challenges, difficult classroom dynamics, and institutional constraints form winding corridors with no clear exit. In the moment, such emotions may appear as obstacles to be fought or suppressed, but without an inner 'thread', teachers risk becoming trapped in cycles of stress or burnout.

The 'red thread' in teaching can be seen as the capacity for emotional awareness and reflective practice: the deliberate act of staying connected to one's values, purpose, and sources of renewal. Like Ariadne's thread, it does not erase the complexity of the labyrinth – it does not remove the Minotaur – but it offers a way to navigate it without losing oneself. Following this thread means allowing negative emotions to be acknowledged, examined, and integrated, rather than ignored or left to dominate. In teaching, this 'red thread' may be understood as the capacity for self-reflection – the ability to trace one's way back to purpose and professional identity, even in the midst of demanding emotional experiences.

From the perspective of DST, this thread connects the many I-positions a teacher inhabits, allowing internal voices – whether of idealism, self-doubt, or resilience – to enter into dialogue rather than remain locked in conflict. The thread represents the possibility of re-establishing a responsive relationship to the context, even when circumstances seem resistant. Thus, navigating the labyrinth of teaching does not mean eliminating negative emotions, just as Theseus could not avoid the labyrinth itself. Instead, it means learning to move through them with awareness, holding onto a guiding line that keeps the teacher connected to self, others, and the wider world of meaning in which education takes place. This orientation prepares the ground for viewing emotions – especially negative ones – not as threats to be escaped, but as signals and opportunities for transformation.

In the following three accounts are proposed as an example of reflexive treads: the possibility of resonance; the relational receptivity; from distraction to attention.

METHODOLOGY

The accounts used in this chapter were collected during a personal research project aimed at analysing teaching emotions through the collecting of anecdotes (Denzin, 2006; Doecke et al., 2000). The two teachers (one man and one woman: Paul, a 40 years old man, secondary school; Julie, 23 years-old, secondary school) were invited to note and share short, concrete episodes from their professional lives – moments in which emotions, interactions, and self-perceptions were particularly vivid. By bringing these lived experiences along a 3- months into a narrative account, they provide opportunities for reflection.

The two last accounts about teacher education arise from my own experience at the same time – in line with a parallel work of autoethnography (Bochner & Ellis, 2022).

The Possibility of Resonance

In the following the first account by Julie:

> *Each workday, I experience a recurring negative emotion tied to one group among the three French classes I teach. My relationship with this group is strained, and whenever I prepare to teach them, I find myself thinking, 'I have to face them again! Why can't someone else take this group? The other classes behave normally, but this one doesn't!' Almost any event in these lessons tends to trigger a negative reaction within me, which then compounds and grows stronger before the next session.*
>
> *At times, I feel caught in a frustrating cycle of self-pity and dissatisfaction. To address this, I committed to observing these feelings more closely and trying to invest greater emotional energy into my interactions with the group (be open to interactions, smiling more, reply with kindness, be compassionate for their difficulties, reacting with sweetness etc). After some tentative, I was able to begin and end the lessons with a more positive emotional state.*

The teacher is caught in a repetitive cycle of negative internal dialogs, where a conflictual positioning of the self-emerged – between duty and resistance. The results became frustration and self-pity. The sense of agency is threatened, and the capacity for mutual transformation is blocked. However, a subtle shift occurs when she begins to observe the students' emotional state more attentively and chooses to engage with intentional openness, even in small ways. This represents both a dialogical re-positioning ('I can try to relate differently') and the beginnings of a resonant moment, where affect is no longer determined solely by external stimuli, but co-constructed through a more attuned, self-reflective stance. She regains a form of voice and agency (Impedovo, 2021).

Relational Receptivity

In the following, one anecdotical episode by Paul:

> *Yesterday morning, I felt a strong sense of judgement towards some colleagues who were engaged in speaking negatively about others' actions.*
>
> *Despite my prejudice towards one of these colleagues, I approached them with gentleness and genuine openness, even though I disagreed with their point of view. I attempted to interact in order to make my request, and the interaction turned out to be calm and serene, rather than merely a transactional exchange.*

This anecdote portrays a moment of internal judgement towards a colleague, reflecting a dialogical tension between an 'I-position' of moral disapproval and another 'I' capable of empathy, openness, and relational receptivity. She chose to override initial judgement and interact differently. This represents a dialogical movement towards integration, where conflicting internal voices are not denied, but held in creative tension. The deliberate shift transforms a potentially mute or antagonistic interaction into a genuinely relational experience. The communicative tone changes: the request is no longer transactional but becomes an opportunity for presence. This shift from judgement to relational attention marks the emergence of a resonant quality in everyday professional life.

From Distraction to Attention

The next account by Julie exemplifies how routine in professional interactions can become emotionally flattened. Moving from distraction to emotions could help to improve state:

> *This year, I became aware of how my start of the day at work followed a predictable rhythm: greeting the colleague in the reception; giving the secretary a document to copy; and collecting sheets to distribute later to my students. These initial 10 minutes of my day had settled into a monotonous routine.*
>
> *After receiving some suggestions from my mentor, I tried to change it – not just to reach a better emotional state for me but also for my colleagues.*
>
> *I started to be more attentive to their emotional states, wondering if they appear sad, tired, stressed etc. This deliberate attention helped me avoid falling back into quick actions to be done.*
>
> *I was looking to find more connections with my colleagues. Indeed, I discovered that even the simplest daily tasks could offer a sense of fulfilment, helping me to start the day with more positive emotions.*

The teacher describes a mini-shifts from a cold relationship to a more active affective and engagement. What once seemed ordinary now holds the potential for transformation – not because the external circumstances changed, but because the mode of relating to them was altered. This exemplifies micro-resonance, a form of everyday relational vitality.

In dialogical terms, this reflects a dominant habitual self-position, where the self-enacts pre-scripted behaviours that lack reflective engagement. However, setting a new internal intention – to be more attentive to both her own emotions and those of others - facilitates a new dialogical positioning. Here, the self-reclaims authorship of its positioning and creates space for new internal dialogs.

Across the three short narrative accounts, we observe how professional practice becomes a site of inner dialogue (Fossa, 2022) and potential resonance, even in moments of tension, repetition, or fatigue -characterised by disconnection and judgement). The teachers emerge not merely reacting but engaging in a renovated (temporary) reconfiguration of their relationship to others and to themselves.

In the following section, we report two accounts by teacher-education context.

OVERCAMING THE STRUGGLE

In the following, I recollect two anecdotes about my practice as teacher educators engaged in self-inquiry.

We can retrace the interplay of multiple internal 'I-positions' – the I as a good teacher, the I as responsible and efficient, the I in doubt, and the emerging ques-

> *In my work as a teacher educator, I have long identified with the image of being thorough, dependable, and fully committed. I take care to complete every task with precision and punctuality, and this consistency has earned me a reputation as someone who can always be relied upon.*
>
> *Over the years, this perception has become more than just feedback – it has fused with my professional identity, shaping the way I see myself. I realized that I often gauge my own worth through the lens of this role, looking for subtle cues from others to confirm that I still embody it.*
>
> *One morning, when a colleague invited volunteers for an additional project, I made an unexpected choice: I declined.*
>
> *In the past, I would have stepped forward without hesitation. This small act unsettled me, stirring feelings of guilt and worry about appearing less committed in the eyes of my colleagues. Yet, the moment also revealed how tightly I hold onto the 'model teacher' script – and how challenging it is to act outside of it.*

tions and repositions between external validation and internal autonomy.

The habitual enactment – one shaped by social feedback and institutional expectations – has become both a source of pride and a psychological constraint. The decision not to volunteer, though seemingly minor, marks a moment of rupture: the emergence of a counter-position that resists the habitual script and introduces ambiguity, vulnerability, and the potential for change. In the second account, the shift becomes more intentional.

In the following, the second account:

The account testimony how my move is dictated by external demands to a felt connection to the moment (Rosa, 2019). It is also an act of resistance

> *Normally, I move through a set of exams with a sense of haste, driven by an inner push to finish quickly – an urgency often tied less to the work itself and more to how my efficiency might be perceived by others. This time, I paused to question that impulse:*
>
> *What lies behind this constant drive for speed? Why is efficiency so bound up with my sense of worth?*
>
> *I began to imagine another way of working – one guided by a genuine interest in the quality of the task, and even joyful in the process. Free from the mental noise of performance and recognition, I noticed how this small shift opened space for calm engagement and care.*

to the instrumental rationality that often governs educational environments. As we lose attachment to the label of the 'good teacher,' we open space for more authentic, ethical, and joyful ways of being in the profession. These processes often involve the manifestation of epiphanies and the surfacing of implicit assumptions (Denzin, 1989; Ellis & Bochner, 2006).

Together, these narratives illustrate a moving to a reflexive awareness.

CONCLUSION

The figure of the teacher emerging from these narratives is not one of passive adaptation to institutional norms, nor of heroic perfection in a neoliberal system (Ling & Livingston, 2023). Rather, it is a teacher engaged in a daily, often invisible, struggle – a struggle to reconcile internal expectations, external demands, and the desire for meaningful, embodied presence in their professional life. The struggle is not only with structural pressures but also with deeply internalized narratives about what it means to be 'good', 'effective', or 'diligent'. These narratives are reinforced by institutional cultures, collegial feedback, and performance-oriented discourses that valorise visibility, productivity, and compliance (Breeze & Taylor, 2020).

In the narrative accounts of the teacher and teacher educators' narrative accounts, we recognise the teacher as an agent of struggle – as engaged in the ethical and emotional labour of becoming (Benesch & Prior, 2023; de Kadt & Jawitz, 2018). This includes confronting internalized ideals, negotiating the dissonance between institutional expectations and personal values, and experimenting with new ways of inhabiting professional identity. Such struggle becomes not a sign of weakness or failure but of vitality – the pulse of an ongoing resonant relationship with the world (Rosa, 2019). Resonance here does not require agreement or emotional harmony, but a willingness to engage meaningfully, despite difference. Thus, the teacher as an agent of struggle is one who does not merely cope with or conform to professional demands, but who reflects, repositions, and reimagines their relationship to work (Way et al., 2015). The teacher's decision to resist certain expectations, to question emotional automatisms, and to reconfigure their sense of agency can be seen as micro-acts that challenge the neoliberal rationalities often embedded in educational systems.

Adopting a perspective centred on emotion and identity on professional development can empower teachers to act upon their own intentions in ways that transform their realities and allow for the enactment of their authentic modes of being-in-the-world (Van Lier, 2008). In this way, it is possible to embody a form of professional becoming that resists closure, embraces vulnerability, and affirms the possibility of a more humane and resonant educational practice.

NOTE

1. https://en.wikipedia.org/wiki/Theseus Theseus was a divine hero in Greek mythology, famous for slaying the Minotaur. The myths surrounding Theseus, his journeys, exploits, and friends, have provided material for storytelling throughout the ages. The most famous legend about Theseus is his slaying of the Minotaur, half man and half bull.

REFERENCES

Beauchamp, C. (2015). Reflection in teacher education: Issues emerging from a review of current literature. *Reflective Practice, 16*(1), 123–141. https://doi.org/10.1080/14623943.2014.982525

Benesch, S., & Prior, M. T. (2023). Rescuing "emotion labor" from (and for) language teacher emotion research. *System, 113,* 102995.

Bochner, A. P., & Ellis, C. (2022). Why autoethnography? *Social Work and Social Sciences Review, 23*(2), 8–18.

Breeze, M., & Taylor, Y., (2020). Feminist collaborations in higher education: Stretched across career stages. *Gender and Education, 32*(3), 412–428. https://doi.org/10.1080/09540253.2018.1471197

Cannella, G. S., & Koro-Ljungberg, M. (2017). Neoliberalism in higher education: Can we understand? Can we resist and survive? Can we become without neoliberalism? *Cultural Studies↔ Critical Methodologies, 17*(3), 155–162.

de Kadt, E., & Jawitz, J. (2018). Exploring discomfort and care in the experience of a national academic staff development programme. *Critical Studies in Teaching and Learning, 6*(2), 21–39. https://doi.org/10.14426/cristal.v6i2.152

del Cerro Santamaría, G. (2020). Challenges and drawbacks in the marketisation of higher education within neoliberalism. *Review of European Studies, 12,* 22.

Denzin, N. K. (1989). *Interpretive biography.* SAGE.

Denzin, N. K. (2006). *Analytic autoethnography, or déjà vu all over again.* 4, 419–428.

do Mar Pereira, M. (2016). Struggling within and beyond the performative university: Articulating activism and work in an "academia without walls". In *Women's studies international forum* (Vol. *54,* pp. 100–110). Pergamon.

Doecke, B., Brown, J., & Loughran, J. (2000). Teacher talk: The role of story and anecdote in constructing professional knowledge for beginning teachers. *Teaching and Teacher Education, 16*(3), 335–348.

Ellis, C., & Bochner, A. P. (2006). Analyzing analytic autoethnography: An autopsy. *Journal of Contemporary Ethnography, 35*(4), 429–449.

Falsafi, L., & Coll, C. (2011). La construcción de la identidad de aprendiz: Coordenadas espacio-temporales. In J. I. Pozo & C. Monereo (Eds.), *La identidad en Psicología de la Educación: necesidad, utilidad ylímites* (pp. 77–98). Narcea.

Ferrare, J. J., & Hora, M. T. (2014). Cultural models of teaching and learning in math and science: Exploring the intersections of culture, cognition, and pedagogical situations. *The Journal of Higher Education, 85*(6), 792–825.

Fossa, P. (Ed.). (2022). *New perspectives on inner speech.* Springer.

Giroux, H. A. (2014). *Neoliberalism's war on higher education.* Haymarket Books.

Hermans, H. J. M. (2013). The dialogical self in education: Introduction. *Journal of Constructivist Psychology, 26*(2), 81–89. https://doi.org/10.1080/10720537.2013.759018

Hermans, H. J. M., & Hermans-Konopka, A. (2010). *Dialogical self theory: Positioning and counter-positioning in a globalizing society.* Cambridge University Press.

Impedovo, M. A. (2021). *Identity and teacher professional development: A reflective, collaborative and agentive learning journey.* Springer Nature.

Ling, L., & Livingston, K. (2023). *Universities in times of crisis and disruption: Dislocated complexity.* Routledge.

Maisuria, A., & Helmes, S. (2019). *Life for the academic in the neoliberal university.* Routledge.

Nixon, E., & Scullion, R. (2022). Academic labour as professional service work? A psychosocial analysis of emotion in lecturer–student relations under marketization. *Human Relations, 75*(9), 1798–1823.

Rosa, A., & Valsiner, J. (2018). The human psyche lives in semiospheres. In *The Cambridge handbook of sociocultural psychology* (Vol. 2, pp. 13–34). https://doi.org/10.1017/9781316662229

Rosa, H. (2019). *Resonance: A sociology of our relationship to the world.* Polity Press.

Roth, S., & Erstad, O. (2016). Positional identities in educational transitions: Connecting contemporary and future trajectories among multiethnic girls. *Ethnography and Education, 11*(1), 57–73. https://doi.org/10.1080/17457823.2015.1040044

Shahjahan, R. A. (2020). On 'being for others': Time and shame in the neoliberal academy. *Journal of Education Policy, 35*(6), 785–811.

Van Lier, L. (2008). Ecological-semiotic perspectives on educational linguistics. In *The handbook of educational linguistics* (pp. 596–605). Wiley-Blackwell.

Vassilieva, J., & Zavershneva, E. (2020). Vygotsky's height psychology: Reenvisioning general psychology in dialogue with the humanities and the arts. *Review of General Psychology, 24*(1), 18–30. https://doi.org/10.1177/1089268020902723

Way, A. K., Zwier, R. K., & Tracy, S. J. (2015). Dialogic interviewing and flickers of transformation: An examination and delineation of interactional strategies that promote participant self-reflexivity. *Qualitative Inquiry, 21*(8), 1–12.

CHAPTER 9

ART TO BE A TEACHER: A ROLE TO PLAY

ABSTRACT

This chapter explores the performative perspective of theatre as a framework for rethinking teacher identity, presence, and professional becoming. Drawing on dialogical self-theory, emphasis is placed on the teacher's entry into a creative state in which presence, reflection, and responsiveness to students coexist. The lived experience expressed in three reflective accounts condensates a movement into becoming, where multiple inner voices are negotiated and reconfigured in the act of teaching. The role of teaching is interpreted as authorial emergence in encounter – with students, the self, and the unpredictability of classroom life. This approach calls for teacher education practices that support the poetic dimensions of pedagogical presence.

Keywords: Theatre; teacher identity; presence; dialogical self-theory; play; art

INTRODUCTION

Teaching is increasingly recognized as an emotionally demanding and psychologically complex profession (Tuxford & Bradley, 2015). Research consistently identifies high levels of stress, burnout, and emotional exhaustion among teachers, especially in the early stages of their careers (Hargreaves, 1998; Kyriacou, 2001). These stressors are not merely the result of workload or administrative burden but often stem from deeper tensions within the

Teacher Dialogical Self, pages 103–112

doi:10.1108/978-1-80686-957-220261010

teacher's lived experience of the role: the constant negotiation between authenticity and professionalism, control and improvisation, emotional involvement and institutional expectations (Rais et al., 2023). Adopting the invitation of Biesta (2023) that requires 'artistry' from teachers, the metaphor of the teacher as an actor – or even as a clown – offers a lens for examining the polyphonic nature of teacher identity.

The classroom becomes both a stage and a mirror: a space where teachers should be present, responsive, and often improvisational, while also carrying the weight of performance and surveillance. By integrating performative perspectives such as 'the inner alter' in dialogue (Marková, 2006), this chapter proposes an alternative reading of teacher stress – not as a failure of resilience, but as a sign of depth and complexity in the process of professional becoming. In doing so, we advocate educational practices that foreground reflexivity, creative presence, and dialogical positioning as resources for sustainable, embodied pedagogy (Impedovo, 2021). Finally, we consider how the role of the theatre could be brought into the teacher's inner landscape to help to open new I-positions.

The chapter is structured as follows. It begins with a theoretical discussion on performative perspectives and the Dialogical Self. Here, the teacher is understood not as a singular voice, but as a dynamic constellation of 'I-positions' negotiating with internalised norms, student expectations, and the unpredictable emotional texture of classroom life (Valsiner, 2007, 2024). Embracing a playful approach, readers are then invited to select one of three areas of interest: how to move between old and new role; how to embrace positions; how to regulate emotions.

Finally, the chapter addresses the tension between the demand for professional consistency and the desire to act from a more personal and authentic stance.

Theatre and the Dialogical Self

The etymology of the word theatre, derived from the Greek theáomai (θεάομαι) – 'to observe' – provides a compelling entry point into understanding human psychological functioning.

Theatre, as a site of amplified observation, not only represents physical action on a stage but also symbolises the reflective dimension of inner life. It allows for the externalisation and dramatic re-enactment of internal conflicts, aspirations, and contradictions – processes that are central to dialogical self-theory. From this perspective, theatre becomes more than a cultural form: it functions as a metaphor for the self as a stage upon which various 'I-positions' emerge, interact, conflict, and evolve. In Valsiner's view, the self is not a unified or static entity but a dynamic system of semiotic positions – a self-in-dialogue. These positions can be inhabited, challenged, or transformed through interaction with others or through symbolic mediation (Valsiner, 2007). The theatrical process – particularly the adoption of roles, voices, and expressive forms – mirrors the psychological movement of taking on new I-positions, allowing the subject to step outside of the habitual and inhabit alternative perspectives (Cunha et al., 2012).

In this light, Shakespeare (1603/2003) famous assertion that the purpose of acting is 'to hold, as 'twere, the mirror up to nature' (Hamlet, III.2) resonates deeply with dialogical Self theory. The stage reflects not only the external moral and social world but also the plurality of the self, made visible through performative enactment. The actor, like the self, moves between positions – hero, fool, victim, observer – each offering a different voice in the internal dialogue. This mirrors what Valsiner describes as the movement from 'positioning' to 'counter-positioning' and towards 'meta-positioning', a developmental trajectory within the dialogical architecture of the self.

Moreover, theatre's capacity to evoke curiosity, ambiguity, and emotional dissonance aligns with Valsiner's understanding of semiotic tension as a driver of development. The dramatic space creates what he might call a 'field of promoted development' (Valsiner, 1997) – a liminal zone in which new meanings can emerge, not through resolution, but through sustained tension and dialogue between conflicting positions. Thus, assuming a theatrical stance – whether in performance or in pedagogical reflection – can be understood as an act of psychological positioning (Impedovo, 2025). It enables the subject to observe themselves as both actor and spectator, internal and external, known and unknown. In this dialogical perspective, a shift in awareness is not merely a cognitive insight but a semiotic and performative reconfiguration of the self: to play a role is to inhabit a new voice, and in doing so, to invite transformation.

THE TEACHER AS ACTOR IN ENCOUNTER

Human beings have created an interesting form of 'reflection of their own being' (Valsiner, 2024, p. 25), in which can be viewed as dramatic performers on their own personal stage.

In educational theory and practice, the metaphor of theatre has long provided a rich lens for reimagining the teacher's role – not as a mere transmitter of content, but as a presence in encounter. This perspective foregrounds the teacher's capacity to inhabit multiple pedagogical positions with authenticity and responsiveness. Crucially, this creative stance is not a performance delivered to students, but a shared, emergent field of interaction in which both teacher and learners act as co-authors of the moment. Drawing on Marková's (2003; 2016) work, intersubjectivity and dialogicality are understood here as foundational conditions for the constitution of the self. Teaching, in this light, entails engaging with the inner alter – the multiplicity of voices within the self – as an improvised dramaturgy of positioning and repositioning. Such improvisation is enacted in the living presence of students, attuned to the contingencies and affordances of the here and now. In this view, gestures, silences, spatial movements, and embodied reactions are not ancillary to teaching but integral to the pedagogical event. The classroom thus becomes a performative space in which attention is cultivated – a noticing process to oneself, to students, to the wider social field, and to the inner flow of thought and feeling (Impedovo & Ligorio, 2025; Machková & Rais, 2024).

This approach resists narrow, instrumental notions of teacher identity, embracing instead a polyphonic self – reflexive, responsive, and open to uncertainty. Entering the role of teacher is akin to stepping onto a stage without a fixed script: the work is to co-create presence in real time with students, colleagues, and institutional structures. In this sense, teaching is less a role to be mastered than a space to be inhabited – a space where the teacher learns to embody the role while remaining open to transformation:

> If teaching is an art and, more specifically a 'double art' of craft and wisdom, then it is important that teachers keep working on their own educational 'artistry' , that is, their ability to make situated judgements about educationally desirable ways of acting in the always new situations they encounter. Biesta (2023, p. 277).

The classroom becomes not only a site of instruction but a stage of experimentation, where the central question is not simply how to teach, but how to be while teaching – a distinction that lies at the heart of professional becoming. Professional identity, here, is neither static nor pre-given; it is dialogically formed and continually re-authored through encounters – with students, with institutional expectations, with colleagues, and with one's evolving inner voices.

METHODOLOGY: PUTTING THE TEACHER ROLE INTO PLAY

In this chapter, (see, Chapter 8) the two teachers (one man and one woman: Paul, a 40 years old man, secondary school; Julie, 23 years-old, secondary school) were invited to note and share short, concrete episodes from their professional lives – moments in which emotions, interactions, and self-perceptions were particularly vivid.

Moreover, in this section, I invite the reader to consider teaching not only as a professional function but also as a space for play. Here, 'play' is understood in its pedagogical and relational sense – a dynamic process that allows teachers to move fluidly between different positions, experiment with their professional identity, and open themselves to creative and responsive ways of being in the classroom. By embracing playfulness, teachers can reimagine their role with greater flexibility, emotional presence, and imaginative potential.

Considering this approach, the paper invites a playful reading approach. Here the proposed activity. Three sections are proposed in the following. Follow your curiosity and use the arrows to navigate to the part of the chapter that speaks to you:

- Go to: How to move between old and new role
- Go to: How to embrace positions
- Go to: How to regulate emotions

What would you like to explore next?

How to Move Between Old and New Role

In the following reflective account, there is a narrative account of Julie (26 years-old, secondary school) that show how to move between old and new role:

> *Recently, I wanted to better understand the sources of my stress at work. I began paying closer attention to the situations that create tension for me, and I identified two regular situations.*
>
> *The first is when I see some students struggling for a long time. I begin to fear losing them. My colleagues have reassured me, explaining that it is 'normal' for some students to fall behind. Yet, I still feel as though I must save all my students. However, after stressful episodes that are not good for my health and well-being, I am now trying to resist the impulse to act as their rescuer. I hold back my impulses and wait until the students who are struggling ask for my explicit help or start to help themselves. However, certain situations provoke thoughts such as, 'You're being insensitiv'e'.*
>
> *The second scenario is when I notice how quickly I accept various requests from my colleagues, and how difficult it is for me to decline invitations to help them. So, I find myself stressed due to many little tasks to accomplish. Recently, when a colleague insists on getting a quick answer, I try to wait – not to give in to pressure. I have managed to reply that I need to check my schedule before agreeing.*
>
> *On the same line, during a meeting, I even pretended not to know certain information about a project - to reassure myself I can deal with situations without always being fully informed. When a colleague reminded me of all the details previously discussed, I felt ridiculous. Being well-informed seems to matter a great deal to me. At the same time, this experience showed me that I can allow myself to be professional without always having to be serious and perfect at all costs.*

This account offers an account of internal negotiations when the teacher begins to explore better the reasons for her stress.

One of the central I-positions expressed here is that of the rescuer – a self-ascribed identity marked by a strong impulse to protect and support others, particularly students perceived as vulnerable. The self-talk – 'You're being insensitive' – functions as an internalized evaluative voice, possibly echoing broader cultural or institutional discourses about what a 'good teacher' should be. This voice, however, is met not with uncritical acceptance but with reflexive inquiry, suggesting the development of psychological distancing (Valsiner, 2002): the ability to relate to internal voices as one perspective among many, rather than as a singular pedagogical truth.

The teacher's awareness of this inclination, coupled with her efforts to delay or inhibit immediate action, suggests the emergence of meta-positioning: the ability to reflect on one's own habitual responses and consider alternative modes of engagement – also in a more passive role. This shift signals a movement from reactive behaviour to intentional authorship, as she begins to craft more context-sensitive responses in both her interactions. The discomfort she experiences reveals how certain identity positions are not easily relinquished, especially those tied to perceived credibility. Yet this small moment of 'not-knower' – instead of fast agreement on external requests - paradoxically opens a space for reflexivity: the realization that not knowing or not performing expertise can also be a form of professional agency and creative experimentation. In this light, the classroom (and the staff room) becomes not merely a workplace, but a stage of becoming, where the teacher rehearses, revises, and repositions herself in relation to both others and her own internal figures (Marková, 2016).

How to Embrace Positions

In the following vignette, there is a narrative account by Paul 40 years old man, teacher in secondary school) to how to embrace positions:

> *This week, the school principal asked me to join her in her office and expressed strong concern about the low participation rates in a recent school-wide science initiative.*
>
> *He suggested that I encourage my colleagues to increase student involvement and raise the overall numbers before the end of the term. For nearly half an hour, he went through participation data and comparison graphs.*
>
> *To me, the data did not seem particularly alarming or far from expectations, and I felt a quiet sense of irritation. We continued to discuss and, considering his agitation I chose to be collaborative and receptive rather than critical.*
>
> *I refrained from challenging his interpretation or immediately defending my colleagues, as I might have done in the past. Instead, I worked with him to generate concrete ideas for improvement. This shift in attitude seemed to ease his frustration.*

In the vignette, the interaction of the teacher with his head school principal reveals an internal tension.

We can retrace contrasting I-positions: the 'defender of colleagues', accustomed to counter-arguments and protective justification, and the 'collaborative professional', willing to listen, adapt, and co-construct solutions.

By choosing to inhabit the latter position, the teacher shifted the tone of the exchange and opened space for new relational dynamics. This shift can be understood as moving between internal voices – one ready to resist, the other curious to engage – which coexist and influence decision-making in professional contexts. In this case, the deliberate choice to suspend immediate resistance enabled a more constructive and creative interaction. The enactment of an alternative Self – flexible, and responsive instead of negative – illustrates how professional identity can be expanded when one dares to experiment with new positions in the inner dialogue.

How to Regulate Emotions

In the following vignette, there is second narrative account by Paul to how to regulate emotions:

> *One afternoon, I received an official email from the school board stating that a parent had raised concerns about the feedback I provided on her son's assessment test.*
>
> *She claimed that my comments were unnecessarily harsh and might have discouraged her son from pursuing the subject. Shortly afterwards, I was asked to submit a written account explaining my evaluation process. This situation unsettled me and triggered a strong emotional response throughout the day.*
>
> *However, to my own surprize, the day after, I approached the matter with an unusual sense of calm. Although it was the first time I had been challenged in this way, I did not allow myself to be absorbed by my stress.*
>
> *Instead, I concentrated on the explanation requested: I prepared a clear and detailed report, provided the necessary documentation. I was happy to maintain professionalism without letting stress dominate myself.*

In the lived experience, the teacher fosters the ability to adjust emotional responses in real time, maintaining composure and intentionality. He moved from confusion to a proactive voice that brought him to manage the conflicting situations.

This negative experience underscores the potential of emotional awareness and regulation for both personal well-being and effective classroom management (Jennings, 2016; Yee & Bailenson, 2007). Developing such awareness enables teachers to manage emotions proactively – before they negatively affect pedagogical presence.

Attentiveness of this kind allows teachers to adapt their instructional strategies to the emotional needs of the moment (Brackett & Rivers, 2014). Over time, such practice contributes to emotional resilience and the cultivation of a supportive learning environment (Sutton & Wheatley, 2019).

For concluded, the lived experience expressed in three accounts condensates a movement into becoming, where multiple inner voices are negotiated and reconfigured in the act of teaching.

BETWEEN AUTHENTICITY AND A ROLE TO PLAY

In educational practice, a persistent tension exists between the demand for professional consistency and the desire to act from a more personal and authentic side. Teachers are often expected to perform a socially codified role – embodying authority, control, and structure – while also being encouraged to engage relationally, sensitively, and authentically with students (Palmer, 1998; van Manen, 1991). This tension between authenticity and role forms a central axis of pedagogical reflection and can be reimagined through a performative and 'artistry' perspective (Biesta, 2023).

As an illustration, the figure of the clown offers a compelling metaphor for professional growth. In clowning, the performer embraces vulnerability, responds to the unexpected, and plays with ambiguity rather than trying to control it.

Just as the clown navigates the stage with sensitivity and humour, the teacher could navigate the meeting with an adaptive presence – able to hold back, observe, and act from a place of openness rather than defensiveness. The alive attention is on the nuances of the moment: attuned to subtle shifts in atmosphere, receptive to emotional undercurrents, and open to the improvised co-creation of meaning.

To inhabit the teacher-clown position is not to reject professionalism, but to reconfigure it through a more embodied, poetic, and relational lens. The clown does not wear a mask to conceal the self but rather to reveal the fragility and vulnerability of the human condition. In doing so, the clown paradoxically enables a more authentic encounter between teacher and learner – a relational space where the boundaries between the personal and the professional become more porous (Morin, 2004). From this perspective, performance is not a denial of authenticity but a medium of connection (Goffman, 1959). When the teacher makes room for humour, play, and even moments of failure – when they risk being seen in their emotional or imperfect dimensions – they model a form of presence that is deeply human. This balancing act opens a pedagogical space that is both intentional and improvisational, structured and spontaneous (Boal, 1992; Lecoq, 2002). In classroom dynamics, students who assume the role of the 'class clown' are frequently marginalised. Their expressive energy is often perceived as a threat to order and efficiency. Yet such students may be enacting the archetypal figure of the trickster, long recognized across cultures as a liminal agent who disrupts norms, provokes thought, and opens space for new meanings (Hyde, 1998). Rather than suppressing this presence, the teacher-clown learns to listen – to engage the trickster not as a disciplinary problem but as a pedagogical invitation. By embracing this approach, the classroom becomes a stage for shared vulnerability, where laughter and confusion are not avoided but explored as part of the learning process.

Through playfulness, the teacher engages in the ethical play – a mode of being that honours the complexity of human interaction, resists rigid categorisation, and opens the classroom to surprize, emotion, and co-construction.

CONCLUSION

Acknowledging the role of play disrupts the traditional logic of control and conformity. To teach, then, is not only to inform, but to risk, to improvise, and to be affected. Furthermore, teacher education should therefore make space for the development of inner-outer dialogue, embodying a pedagogy that is at once sensitive, creative, and critically awake to the poetic dimensions of human encounter.

REFERENCES

Biesta, G. (2023). Outline of a theory of teaching: What teaching is, what it is for, how it works, and why it requires artistry. In *Theorizing teaching: Current status and open issues* (pp. 253–280). Springer International Publishing.

Boal, A. (1992). *Games for actors and non-actors* (A. Jackson, Trans.). Routledge.

Brackett, M. A., & Rivers, S. E. (2014). Emotion regulation in educational settings. In J. J. Gross (Ed.), *Handbook of emotion regulation* (2nd ed., pp. 492–507). Guilford Press.

Cunha, C., Salgado, J., & Gonçalves, M. M. (2012). The dialogical self in movement: Reflecting on methodological tools for the study of the dynamics of change and stability in the self. In E. Abbey & S. Surgan (Eds.), *Emerging methods in psychology* (pp. 65–100). Transaction Publishers.

Goffman, E. (1959). *The presentation of self in everyday life*. Anchor Books.

Hargreaves, A. (1998). The emotional practice of teaching. *Teaching and Teacher Education, 14*(8), 835–854.

Hyde, L. (1998). *Trickster makes this world: Mischief, myth, and art.* Farrar, Straus and Giroux.

Impedovo, M. A. (2021). *Identity and teacher professional development: A reflective, collaborative and agentive learning journey*. SPRINGER BRIEF. https://link.springer.com/book/10.1007/978-3-030-71367-6

Impedovo, M., & Ligorio, M. B. (2025). Teacher practices observation enriched by collective discussion: Teacher noticing as I-position. *Journal of Constructivist Psychology*, 1–24.

Impedovo, M. (2025). Mirroring the self through Hamlet affective aesthetic experience. *Integrative Psychological and Behavioral Science, 59*(3), 1–16.

Jennings, P. A. (2016). *Mindfulness for teachers: Simple skills for peace and productivity in the classroom.* W. W. Norton & Company.

Kyriacou, C. (2001). Teacher stress: Directions for future research. *Educational Review, 53*(1), 27–35.

Lecoq, J. (2002). *The moving body: Teaching creative theatre* (D. Bradby, Trans.). Routledge.

Machková, M., & Rais, M. (2024). On the hidden potential of public solitude, Part I: Ivan Vyskočil's theatre as encounter. *Stanislavski Studies, 12*(1), 69–86. https://doi.org/10.1080/20567790.2023.2286600

Marková, I. (2003). Constitution of the self: Intersubjectivity and dialogicality. *Culture & Psychology, 9*(3), 249–259.

Marková, I. (2006). On 'the inner alter'in dialogue. *International Journal for Dialogical Science, 1*(1), 125–147.

Marková, I. (2016). *The dialogical mind: Common sense and ethics.* Cambridge University Press.

Morin, E. (2004). *Seven complex lessons in education for the future.* UNESCO.

Palmer, P. J. (1998). *The courage to teach: Exploring the inner landscape of a teacher's life.* Jossey-Bass.

Rais, M., Eliášová, M., Le Quesne, L., & Hamilton, J. (2023). Improvisation as practicing trust: Interview with Julyen Hamilton. *Theatralia, 26*(2), 197–203.

Shakespeare, W. (1603/2003). The tragedy of Hamlet, Prince of Denmark. In S. Greenblatt (Ed.), *The Norton shakespeare* (2nd ed., pp. 1660–1730). W. W. Norton & Company.

Sutton, R. E., & Wheatley, K. F. (2019). Teachers' emotions and teaching: A review of the literature and directions for future research. *Educational Psychology Review, 31*(2), 299–317.

Tuxford, L. M., & Bradley, G. L. (2015). Emotional job demands and emotional exhaustion in teachers. *Educational Psychology, 35*(8), 1006–1024.

Valsiner, J. (1997). *Culture and the development of children's action: A theory of human development* (2nd ed.). Wiley.

Valsiner, J. (2007). *Culture in minds and societies: Foundations of cultural psychology.* SAGE.

Valsiner, J. (2024). *Dynamic semiosis.* Springer.

Valsiner, J. (2002). Forms of dialogical relations and semiotic autoregulation within the self. In H. Hermans & G. Dimaggio (Eds.), *The dialogical self in psychotherapy* (pp. 67–82). Brunner-Routledge.

van Manen, M. (1991). *The tact of teaching: The meaning of pedagogical thoughtfulness.* SUNY Press.

Yee, N., & Bailenson, J. (2007). The Proteus effect: The effect of transformed self-representation on behavior. *Human Communication Research, 33*(3), 271–290.

CHAPTER 10

TEACHER REFLEXIVITY: BECOMING IN THE IRREVERSIBLE TIME

ABSTRACT

This chapter explores teacher professional development through the lens of temporality. It argues that teaching and learning unfold within cyclical temporal patterns – daily routines, weekly rhythms, and yearly academic cycles – that shape both professional identity and pedagogical practice. Rather than viewing growth as a linear acquisition of skills, the chapter reframes development as a dynamic, reciprocal process marked by moments of rupture, discomfort, and surprize. The chapter emphasises the importance of attending to small, situated events – moments where embodied interactions, emotional intensities, and relational dynamics converge to catalyze transformation. It advocates for an understanding of inquiry and professional development as generative, open spaces where teachers continuously remake themselves, their relationships, and their educational environments.

Keywords: Teacher; professional development; reflexivity; time; dialogical self theory

INTRODUCTION: THE TEMPORALITIES OF TEACHING

Teaching is lived experience and practice within a dense web of temporal structures. Days unfold according to timetables; weeks are punctuated by recurring duties and meetings; academic years trace the arc from

Teacher Dialogical Self, pages 113–121

doi:10.1108/978-1-80686-957-220261011

anticipation to closure. Over time, these cycles become embedded in teachers' routines, shaping their professional practices. Yet these temporalities are not neutral. The daily repetition of tasks can foster stability and predictability, but it can also produce a kind of automatisation – a narrowing of attention in which gestures, words, and interactions are performed without renewed engagement. The cyclic nature of weeks, semesters, and years offers opportunities for reflection, recalibration, and renewal, but such opportunities should be actively cultivated (Cramer et al., 2023).

To sustain qualitative professional growth (Germanos & Roth, 2024), teachers should learn to confront and work with these temporal patterns. This means recognising the force of certain moments return and using them as openings for transformation. It also means acknowledging the longer arcs of professional life, where the accumulation of experiences, and the rhythms of beginnings and endings, shape deeper shifts in professionalism (Tatto, 2021).

In this chapter, I explore how teachers can engage with a reflexivity about both the immediacy of the present moment and the cyclical temporality of educational work. Professional learning emerges in the smallest, most situated moments – moments that open pathways to re-imagining practice. The chapter is structured as follows. The theoretical framework is grounded in the notion of becoming in time and the process of reflexivity – conceived as a deliberate revisiting of one's professional path. This is followed by a reflective account and a playful activity designed to resonate with lived experiences.

BECOMING IN THE IRREVERSIBLE TIME

The concept of Dasein, introduced by Heidegger (1927/1962), refers to the condition of 'being there' and is fundamental for understanding human existence as inherently temporal. Within this view, time is not an external entity but is embedded in human subjectivity. Nevertheless, Dasein is not confined to subjective experience alone; it also points to a mode of being that resists reduction to purely individual consciousness. Drawing from the philosophical legacies of Husserl, Heidegger, Bergson, and Mead, Valsiner (2008, 2018) articulates existence as a process of becoming. This framework integrates Bergson's idea of irreversibility, which implies that time unfolds in a non-repetitive, forward-moving manner (del Río & Molina, 2022). The present moment is understood as a dynamic threshold where past experiences and future possibilities intersect. This intersection creates a tension between what has already passed and what has yet to come, thereby giving rise to novelty and transformation (Valsiner, 2018). In this continuous process of becoming, human experience is marked by an intrinsic uncertainty about what lies ahead (De Luca Picione &

Lozzi, 2021; Valsiner, 2020). Temporal experience is thus characterised not by mere adaptation to external conditions, but by transformation – a process marked by emergence, ambiguity, and the creation of new meaning: 'All psychological events are temporal in nature, while the meaning-making mind presents these as framed by different static time units' (Valsiner, 2024, p. 4).

Self-reflection enables individuals to revisit past experiences as distinct events that disrupt the flow of everyday life. These moments are perceived as discontinuities that separate a 'before' from an 'after', thereby fostering the emergence of new meanings and future-oriented action (Zittoun, 2006). This existential uncertainty is situated within the interplay of meaning, communication, and relational encounters – with oneself, with others, and with the material world (Couzens Hoy, 2009; Molina et al., 2017). Through semiosis – the process by which meaning is constructed via signs – the self is continuously shaped and reshaped. Semiosis allows for the reinterpretation of past experiences in relation to imagined futures, maintaining a constant openness to change. The notion of chronogenesis, advanced by authors such as Sato and Valsiner (2010), underscores this generative temporal dimension. It reflects how individuals organise experiences and meanings in the present, while projecting forward into possible futures shaped by imagined attractors. These attractors provide a directional pull, influencing the present moment and its unfolding (Valsiner, 2008). Bergson's (1959) idea of duration encapsulates the fullness and continuity of lived temporality. From this perspective, time is not measured mechanically but experienced qualitatively. Irreversibility, as emphasised by Sato and Valsiner (2010), disrupts the notion of a linear temporal order: while the past is fixed along a singular trajectory, the future remains open-ended, offering a spectrum of potential outcomes and emergent states.

In the following a reflexive journaling note about the temporality and the becoming in time.

Cyclical End and New Beginnings

The time is a central factor in the teacher's professional development. In the following, a reflective account on it - inviting to reflexivity:

This year, I have come to understand that transformation in teaching is never one-directional. The effort I invest in my own growth does not remain contained within me; it shapes the classroom, the institutional culture, my colleagues, and my students. The more I return to moments that have marked me – whether they were filled with ease or difficulty – the more I see how they continue to inform my presence now.

In those returns, thought and emotion meet as inseparable companions. Learning emerges not only through deliberate reasoning, but through the quiet undercurrents of what is felt, hoped for, and feared. Some experiences recall the satisfaction of things working well, the spark that draws attention and energises action. Others carry the sting of discomfort – times when I felt out of place or uncertain. These, too, are vital. They unsettle fixed patterns, interrupt the predictable, and open cracks where something new can enter.

Such revisiting changes how I see the present. What once felt like error may reveal itself as a necessary step, what seemed insignificant can become luminous when placed in a different light. This shifting of perspective is not a denial of difficulty, but an enlargement of possibility: building from what is already vital while allowing the troubling to deepen my understanding.

Professional growth, from this view, is not a checklist of techniques to be acquired, but a living process shaped by the capacity to remain open – to be moved, challenged, and even surprized by the unexpected. Some of the richest moments in teaching have arrived unplanned: in a student's sudden insight, in my own unanticipated response, or in an encounter that shows me a part of myself I had not yet met.

Looking back across the year, I sense that growth lies in preparing the ground for such surprizes. This means loosening the hold of overly rigid plans so that new paths can emerge, allowing the present to converse with what has come before. If I could stand beside the teacher I was twelve months ago, I would not offer a map. I would simply say: Let the process be slow. Not everything will make sense right away, and that is where the most enduring learning often begins.

CYCLICAL REFLEXIVITY

Considering the above perspective of becoming in the irreversible time, teacher professional development does not unfold in a straight line; it is more akin to a spiral, where experiences recur and they need different depths of reflection.

Reflection is central to teacher education, as they enable teachers to critically examine both their practices and the underlying assumptions shaping them.

Early approaches, such as those of Mezirow (1991) and Brookfield (1995), emphasised critical reflection as a way to question taken-for-granted beliefs and to foster more conscious pedagogical choices. Phenomenological perspectives (e.g., Biesta, 2016; Polanyi, 2009) remind us that reflection is always partial, shaped by tacit knowledge and relations with the world.

In more recent discussions, reflection is linked to personal epistemology, understood as teachers' beliefs about knowledge. This epistemic dimension allows reflection to move beyond situational analysis towards questioning the foundations of teaching practices (Feucht et al., 2017).

According to Cramer et al. (2023) we need the sustain of a meta-reflexivity: reflection in the sense of multi perspectivity utilises different perspectives to look at one issue; meta-reflexivity asks how reflections on multiple issues from multiple perspectives are made in specific contexts. In summary, adopting meta-reflexivity, teachers learn to see their work not only as a sequence of challenges to overcome, but as an evolving field of meaning in which they are active co-creators: 'A meta-reflexive teacher is aware that there is no linear application of theory to practice. Through contrasting engagement with different or even apparently incommensurable (scientific and experience-based) perspectives, meta-reflexivity could be initiated as broadening the perspective on professional practice' (Cramer et al., 2023).

Between the variety of definitions (Clarà, 2015), reflection is here understood as a socio-historically embedded social practice, shaped by dialogical processes of reinterpreting meanings and experiences, which in turn fosters the improvement of action (Wortham, 2006). Reflection emerges first at a microgenetic level, within social interactions, and is later internalized as an individual psychological process (Vygotsky, 1978/2009). Through dialogue with significant others – such as family, colleagues, or teachers – individuals gradually appropriate tools for reflective thinking, mediated by language and other semiotic means, until they can use them autonomously (Wertsch et al., 1993). At a macrogenetic level, reflection is also shaped by broader cultural, social, and institutional discourses. These historically constructed voices, transmitted across contexts, influence how people think and engage in reflexivity, as highlighted in dialogical theories (Bakhtin, 1986).

Through the interplay of multiple voices coexisting, meanings are negotiated and individuals position themselves in relation to different perspectives (Monereo & Hermans, 2023). From a sociocultural perspective, reflection is rooted in action while simultaneously enabling its reconstruction and improvement. It both fosters awareness of the elements that shape activity and supports the transformation of practice through deeper understanding of those elements.

Emphasising the cyclical nature of reflexivity in relation to recurring teaching experiences, the following section introduces a playful activity designed to connect reflection with time and key dimensions of teaching practice.

Game: Cyclical Reflexivity

How to Play:

1. Take a dice (or improvise one online).
2. Roll it once.
3. Match your number to the dimension below.
4. Read the description and ask yourself:

What of it resonates or unsettles me now? What is my understanding of it today?

1. *Experiencing the care in teaching (see, Chapter 2 'Teacher Noticing as Self-Portraiture: Relational Practices')*
   As Tronto (1998) reminds us, care is both an ethical and affective orientation towards others and oneself. It goes beyond empathy or kindness, involving a sustained commitment to students, to one's subject, and to one's own growth. In teaching, care is a form of attentiveness and responsibility that integrates emotional, relational, and professional dimensions.
2. *Experiencing attention (see, The Chapter 3 'The lived experience as professional possibility').* Biesta (2023) has suggested conceptualising teaching as a form to (re)direct the attention of another human being aimed at an 'attention formation'. Attention does not arise automatically – it is invited, guided in concrete situations. Attention re-infuse learning with intention.
3. *Experiencing art (see, The Chapter 4 'Zones of sense: Pathways to Teacher Self')*
   Art can revitalise our gaze, helping us to inhabit the present moment more fully and with greater depth. Soundscapes and photographic images can open how sensory experiences.
4. *Experiencing emotion (The Chapter 8 'Emotion and Teacher Identity')*
   Small shifts – a change in tone, a simple gesture, a striking image, or a provocative question – can reawaken the emotional significance of our work. Emotion, in this sense, is a catalyst for connection and renewed engagement. A teacher's desire – to connect, to inspire, to witness growth – is inseparable from classroom experience and evolving professional identity.
5. *Experiencing the body (Chapter 5 'Exploring the Teacher bodily Self')*
   Bodily gestures are meaningful contributions to both internal and external dialogs. For instance, a student's posture or gaze may convey resistance, curiosity, or vulnerability, prompting specific teacher responses.
6. *Experiencing the playfulness (The Chapter 9 'Art to be a teacher: a role to play')*
   Playfulness in teaching emerges as a pedagogical stance that stimulates creativity and engagement (Holflod, 2022; Sproule et al., 2021). Such moments often disrupt traditional power dynamics, fostering reciprocity between teacher and students (Noddings, 2012). They contribute to a positive emotional climate, which supports motivation and deeper learning.

Loop Back

When you finish, notice which dimension called to you most strongly. Carry your understanding into your next teaching encounter as an active practice of reflexivity – and watch how it changes the way your understanding moves through time.

CONCLUSION: REFLEXIVITY AS A GENERATIVE SPACE FOR NEW UNDERSTANDING

By critically revisiting experiences, teachers open possibilities for reinterpreting their practices, questioning assumptions, and envisioning alternative pathways. In this sense, reflexivity becomes a generative force, fostering both professional growth and the transformation of educational activity. Professional growth is rarely a straight climb; it is a movement through shifting terrains of certainty, doubt, discovery, and renewal. Within the inherent uncertainties of teaching, teachers are constantly called to make informed and ethically grounded decisions that they judge to be appropriate and justified. Cultivating this capacity for reflecting about their practices and their understanding enables teachers to navigate complexity with greater assurance, thereby creating the conditions to enhance development. Professional development, in this sense, is about how we choose to remember, question, and reimagine the path we are walking.

REFERENCES

Bakhtin, M. (1986). *Speech genres and other late essays.* University of Texas Press.

Bergson, H. (1934/1959). *La pensée et le mouvant.* PUF.

Biesta, G. (2016). The rediscovery of teaching: On robot vacuum cleaners, non-egological education and the limits of the hermeneutical world view. *Educational Philosophy and Theory, 48*(4), 374–392. https://doi.org/10.1080/00131857.2015.1041442

Biesta, G. (2023). The integrity of education and the future of educational studies. *British Journal of Educational Studies, 71*(5), 493–515.

Brookfield, S. D. (1995). *Becoming a critically reflective teacher.* Jossey-Bass.

Clarà, M. (2015). What is reflection? Looking for clarity in an ambiguous notion. *Journal of Teacher Education, 66*(3), 261–271. https://doi.org/10.1177/0022487114552028

Couzens Hoy, D. (2009). *The time of our lives: A critical history of temporality.* MIT Press.

Cramer, C., Brown, C., & Aldridge, D. (2023). Meta-reflexivity and teacher professionalism: Facilitating multiparadigmatic teacher education to achieve a future-proof profession. *Journal of Teacher Education, 74*(5), 467–480. https://doi.org/10.1177/00224871231162295

De Luca Picione, R., & Lozzi, P. (2021). The uncertainty of future and the dynamics of meaning-making: A semiotic-cultural approach to psychological time. *Integrative Psychological and Behavioral Science, 55*, 741–757.

del Río, M., & Molina, M. (2022). Becoming, time and irreversibility: Rethinking human development through a semiotic cultural lens. *Human Development, 66*(2), 78–90.

Feucht, F. C., Brownlee, J. L., & Schraw, G. (2017). Moving beyond reflection: Reflexivity and epistemic cognition in teaching and teacher education. *Educational Psychologist, 52*(4), 234–241. https://doi.org/10.1080/00461520.2017.1350180

Germanos, E., & Roth, W. M. (2024). Quantitative-cumulative and qualitative-transformational changes in the continuous becoming of teachers. *Outlines. Critical Practice Studies, 25*, 27–49.

Heidegger, M. (1927/1962). *Being and time* (J. Macquarrie & E. Robinson, Trans.). Harper & Row.

Holflod, K. (2022). Voices of playful learning: Experimental, affective and relational perspectives across social education and teacher education. *Journal of Play in Adulthood, 4*(1), 72–91. https://search.informit.org/doi/10.3316/informit.639291576305160

Mezirow, J. (1991). *Transformative dimensions of adult learning.* Jossey-Bass.

Molina, M., Zittoun, T., & Gillespie, A. (2017). Meaning making in transitions: The role of symbolic resources. *Cultural Psychology, 23*(2), 211–232.

Monereo, C., & Hermans, H. (2023). Education and dialogical self: State of art. *Journal for the Study of Education and Development, 46*(3), 445–491. https://doi.org/10.1080/02103702.2023.2201562

Noddings, N. (2012). The caring relation in teaching. *Oxford Review of Education, 38*(6), 771–781. https://doi.org/10.1080/03054985.2012.745047

Polanyi, M. (2009). *The tacit dimension.* University of Chicago Press.

Sato, T., & Valsiner, J. (2010). Dialogue between oneself yesterday and oneself today: A theoretical proposal for a methodology of double self-confrontation. *Forum for Qualitative Social Research, 11*(1). Article 16.

Sproule, L., Walsh, G., & McGuinness, C. (2021). Signalling playfulness: Disguising work as play in the early years' classroom. *International Journal of Play, 10*(3), 228–242. https://doi.org/10.1080/21594937.2021.1959232

Tatto, M. T. (2021). Professionalism in teaching and the role of teacher education. *European Journal of Teacher Education, 44*(1), 20–44.

Tronto, J. C. (1998). An ethic of care. *Generations: Journal of the American society on Aging, 22*(3), 15–20.

Valsiner, J. (2020). *A guided science of the self: Cultural psychology in the world of the future.* Springer.

Valsiner, J. (2018). *Anticipating the future: Concepts and methodological issues.* Springer.

Valsiner, J. (2008). *Culture in minds and societies: Foundations of cultural psychology.* Sage.

Valsiner, J. (2024). *Dynamic semiosis.* Springer.

Vygotsky, L. S. (1978). *Mind in society: Development of higher psychological processes.* Harvard University Press.

Wertsch, J. V., Tulviste, P., & Hagstrom, F. (1993). A sociocultural approach to agency. In *Contexts for learning: Sociocultural dynamics in children's development* (Vol. *23*, pp. 336–356).

Wortham, S. (2006). *Learning identity. The joint emergence of social identification and academic learning.* Cambridge University Press.

Zittoun, T. (2006). *Transitional objects and symbolic resources: Psychological development in times of social change.* Information Age Publishing.

CHAPTER 11

POINTS FOR DEBATE – THE ACT OF PERFORMING TEACHER PROFESSIONAL DEVELOPMENT AND WELLBEING

ABSTRACT

Teaching today unfolds within a landscape marked by both vulnerability and opportunity, where growing shortages and declining morale underscore the urgency of rethinking teacher development as inseparable from well-being and emotional sustainability. Current international reports reveal rising stress, burnout, and attrition, intensified by expanding expectations that often lack adequate structural support. Within this context, the Dialogical Self Theory offers a valuable lens for understanding how identity and well-being emerge through dialogue, reflection, and participation in professional communities. These spaces allow teachers to experiment, reinterpret their roles, and strengthen coherence and belonging. Ultimately, viewing the teacher's self as dialogical reframes professional development as an ongoing relational process, grounded in meaning-making, connection, and the ethical commitment to remain present in the world of education.

Keywords: Professional development; wellbeing; dialogical self; workplace culture; workplace dynamics

---

Teacher Dialogical Self, pages 123–134

doi:10.1108/978-1-80686-957-220261012

TEACHING IN A TIME OF PRECARITY AND POSSIBILITIES

Teaching today unfolds within a paradoxical landscape of precarity and potential (Ana et al., 2020). On one hand, teachers across the world face intensified pressures – administrative overload, policy accountability, and emotional exhaustion – conditions that have been further exacerbated by global crises such as the climatic change and ongoing social inequalities (Day & Gu, 2010; Impedovo, 2021a; OECD, 2021, 2022). On the other hand, education continues to hold the promise of transformation, both personal and collective. Teachers are called upon to navigate between these two poles: sustaining their capacity to care, to create meaning, and to act ethically within conditions that often undermine their very sense of purpose (Hargreaves & Fullan, 2020).

This reflection in this book explore that dynamic space of becoming – a space where the teacher dialogical self emerges as both fragile and generative. Across the 10 chapters, the reader has been invited to inhabit the multiplicity of teacher voices: voices that doubt, resist, hope, and create. In exploring these polyphonic dimensions of the teacher's professional identity, the book argues that professional development cannot be reduced to the acquisition of new skills or the adaptation to institutional mandates. Instead, it should be reimagined as a process of inner dialogue – a dialogical engagement with the self, others, and the world that sustains teachers' sense of agency and belonging.

As educational systems worldwide struggle with teacher shortages and declining morale, it becomes increasingly urgent to reframe professional development not only as a matter of competence but also as a matter of well-being, emotional sustainability, and human flourishing (Schutz et al., 2018). The teacher's self – understood through a dialogical lens (Hermans, 2011) – is never static; it is always in motion, negotiating between internal and external voices, personal desires, and institutional expectations. This movement is both the source of vitality and vulnerability in the profession. To understand and support teacher well-being, therefore, we attend to this inner dialogue: to the stories teachers tell about themselves, to the tensions they hold, and to the meaning-making processes through which they sustain their professional presence.

In this sense, the teacher dialogical self offers a counterpoint to the prevailing neoliber claim. Rather than viewing teachers as deliverers of outcomes, the dialogical perspective situates them as meaning-makers engaged in ongoing negotiation of identity, ethics, and purpose. The chapters of this book have shown that attending to the inner, emotional, and imaginative life of teachers is not a luxury – it is a condition of pedagogical vitality. The question of teacher well-being, therefore, is not peripheral but central to the renewal of education.

The Contemporary Condition of Teachers: Well-Being and Emotional Sustainability

The growing global concern about teacher well-being reflects deeper structural transformations in education. Across Europe and beyond, numerous studies have documented alarming levels of teacher stress, burnout, and attrition (OECD, 2021, 2022; Skaalvik & Skaalvik, 2018). Teaching has become characterised by what some scholars call 'intensification' – an expansion of duties and expectations without corresponding support or recognition. Teachers are expected to be emotionally available, pedagogically innovative, digitally skilled, and culturally responsive – yet often within institutions that provide little space for reflection, collaboration, or self-care. This misalignment produces what Day and Gu (2010) describe as 'moral dissonance', a gap between teachers' professional ideals and the realities of their working conditions.

Well-being, however, cannot be equated merely with the absence of stress or burnout. It entails a deeper sense of coherence and connectedness – a capacity to align one's actions with one's values, to find meaning in daily practices, and to sustain professional identity amidst uncertainty (Ryan & Deci, 2017). For teachers, this coherence is inherently dialogical: it emerges through reflective conversation with self and others, through narrative reconstruction of experience, and through the capacity to reposition oneself in response to shifting contexts (Hermans & Hermans-Konopka, 2010).

From this perspective, teacher well-being is not an individual possession but a relational and narrative achievement. It develops within communities of practice, through shared language and mutual recognition. When teachers are deprived of spaces for authentic dialogue – when their voices are silenced by bureaucratic demands or competitive evaluation – well-being erodes not only as emotional fatigue but as loss of self-understanding. This erosion is a dialogical wound: the interruption of inner conversation that sustains identity coherence (Bakhtin, 1986).

The empirical and narrative inquiries throughout this book illustrate that teachers' well-being is sustained when they can speak and be heard – when their experiences are not merely managed but meaningfully acknowledged. The creative and dialogical processes reopen the space for teachers to reconnect with their inner speech and sense of agency. These forms of inquiry do not merely document teachers' struggles; they reconstitute them as sites of growth and self-understanding.

Recent research aligns with this dialogical interpretation. Studies on emotional labour in teaching highlight how teachers continuously mediate between genuine feelings and institutional expectations (Sturrock, 2022). When this mediation becomes rigid or unacknowledged, emotional exhaustion follows. But when teachers are supported in articulating the multiple voices within – when they can integrate rather than suppress their emotional complexity – new forms of professional authenticity and resilience emerge (Schutz et al., 2018).

Supporting teacher well-being, therefore, means cultivating dialogical ecosystems – educational environments that value inner reflection, relational connectedness, and plural voices. Such ecosystems move beyond individual resilience programs or temporary wellness initiatives; they embed well-being into the ethical and cultural foundations of teacher education. This is particularly urgent in the face of widespread teacher shortages, where systemic responses often focus on recruitment rather than retention, efficiency rather than meaning.

The Crisis of Entry and Maintenance in the Teaching Profession

Across global contexts, the teaching profession is experiencing an unprecedented recruitment and retention crisis. Reports by the OECD (2021, 2022) and United Nations Educational, Scientific and Cultural Organization (UNESCO), (2023) highlight a significant decline in teacher numbers and a growing difficulty in attracting and sustaining qualified professionals, particularly in disadvantaged areas and specialised subjects.

For instance, UNESCO's recent Global Report on Teachers: Addressing Teacher Shortages and Transforming the Profession draws attention to the urgent scale of the challenge: an estimated need for some 44 million additional primary and secondary teachers by 2030 in order to achieve Sustainable Development Goals 4 (inclusive, equitable quality education). The report emphasises that recruitment is only one side of the coin – the other is retention, working conditions, professional status, and the attractiveness of the teaching profession. Similarly, the International Task Force on Teachers for Education 2030 (Teacher Training Framework (TTF)) provides policy briefs and background papers that explicitly link teacher well-being with workforce sustainability. A recent background paper titled Teacher Well-being and the Shaping of Teacher Shortages in Crisis-Affected Contexts emphasises that teacher well-being is coterminous with retention and supply: in crisis contexts, teaching is simultaneously a protective and risk factor in teachers' lives.

In many systems, the average age of teachers is rising, while new entrants leave within the first five years (UNESCO, 2023). The reasons are complex – ranging from workload intensification and low societal recognition to emotional exhaustion and lack of professional autonomy.

While structural factors such as remuneration and policy frameworks are critical, an equally powerful – yet often underexplored – dimension concerns the subjective and relational experience of becoming and remaining a teacher. The processes of entry and maintenance in the profession are not only institutional but also deeply existential and dialogical. They involve the continuous negotiation of identity, purpose, and belonging. When these inner negotiations are unsupported, teachers' sense of coherence disintegrates, leading to disengagement and exit (Day & Hong, 2016; Kelchtermans, 2009).

Early-career teachers often enter the profession with strong moral and relational motivations – a desire to make a difference, to contribute to community, to enact values of care and justice (Dania & Impedovo, 2025). Yet, as they encounter institutional realities – standardized curricula, performative accountability, and administrative overload – these initial motivations may clash with the daily conditions of work. This identity tension becomes a critical determinant of teacher persistence (Dania & Impedovo, 2025). Without supportive structures for dialogue, mentoring, and reflection, the dissonance between personal vocation and institutional expectation leads to attrition.

Retention, therefore, cannot be addressed solely through technical induction programs or financial incentives. What is required is a pedagogical ecology of belonging, where teachers – novice and experienced alike – can articulate their inner voices, encounter others' perspectives, and reconstruct meaning in the face of challenge. The Dialogical Self Theory (DST) provides a conceptual lens for such an ecology. It suggests that teachers' professional selves are composed of multiple 'I-positions' (Hermans, 2011), each carrying its own emotions, values, and voices of others. The vitality of a professional identity depends on the dynamic dialogue among these positions. When external pressures silence certain voices – for instance, the caring self or the creative self – the teacher's dialogical balance becomes precarious, undermining well-being and motivation.

Research on teacher attrition underscores this point. Klassen and Chiu (2011) found that emotional exhaustion and workload predict teachers' intentions to leave more strongly than salary or resources. Similarly, studies by Day and Gu (2010) show that teachers' resilience and commitment are closely linked to their ability to sustain a meaningful identity narrative. The challenge is not only to retain teachers in employment but to sustain them as dialogical, reflective subjects who can continue to see teaching as a site of becoming rather than depletion.

Therefore, rethinking the recruitment and maintenance of teachers involves more than workforce management. It requires rethinking teacher education and professional development as ongoing identity work – as the cultivation of dialogical spaces that affirm teachers as meaning-makers and co-constructors of educational life. This aligns with the ethos of this book: to move from professional development as skill acquisition to professional becoming as dialogical engagement.

From the perspective of professional development and retention, facilitating teachers' active movement within communities is crucial. It transforms isolated work into relational practice, where professional well-being is not an ancillary goal but an integral part of daily engagement. These communities provide scaffolds for sustaining motivation, nurturing agency, and supporting the dynamic process of becoming a teacher. Ultimately, professional well-being is performed, nurtured, and maintained within these shared spaces, where teachers' multiple voices are recognized, harmonised, and amplified.

What do these institutional documents contribute to our conversation about teacher dialogical selves, professional development, and well-being?

Institutional frameworks assert that teacher professional life is not solely a matter of individual commitment, but of conditions: remuneration, workload, autonomy, career pathways, policy support. For example, the United Nations Secretary-General's High-Level Panel on the Teaching Profession states explicitly that decent working conditions, professional autonomy and teacher well-being are foundational to effective teaching and learning. More, the TTF background paper emphasises that teacher shortages are deeply connected with teacher well-being – that is, retention failures are not simply about money or recruitment numbers but about how teachers feel, function and are supported in their professional lives. In effect, the macro-policy domain recognises what our book argues: that professional development extend beyond technique and competency to relational, identity and well-being dimensions.

Yet, institutional frameworks provide leverage for aligning educational development with teacher subjectivity. For example, the Global Report outlines that addressing teacher shortages requires not just quantitative recruitment but qualitative transformation: fostering teachers' professional autonomy, decision-making, collaboration, and recognition. From our dialogical lens, this means institutional policy can support the conditions under which the teacher's many voices engage in creative, ethical, and sustainable dialogue rather than being silenced or narrowed.

Finally, however, these documents also underscore a tension: policy frameworks often remain at the level of structure and metrics, while the lived teacher voice remains largely invisible. The macro-documents emphasise numbers, recruitment targets, salaries, ratios – but less often the narrativised inner life of teachers: their dialogical self, sense of belonging, emotional complexity, aesthetic engagement. This gap points to the core insight of this book: that supporting teacher well-being means building systems that attend to both external conditions and internal dialogs.

In conclusion, in terms of professional development and identity formation, the institutional dimension invites teacher education programmes and school systems to embed the relational, reflective practices we have explored. The convergence of the macro-policy lens and the micro-dialogical lens invites us to re-imagine teacher education and professional development as both social and personal – where teachers navigate their voices, relational positions and becoming within systems designed to care for them.

The Dialogical Self as a Framework for Rethinking Teacher Well-Being

The DST (Hermans, 2011; Hermans & Hermans-Konopka, 2010) offers a framework for understanding and addressing teacher well-being. For teachers, this implies that professional identity and well-being are dialogically constituted through interaction, reflection, and negotiation.

In the context of teaching, dialogicality manifests as the inner conversation between multiple professional voices: the 'I as carer', 'I as evaluator', 'I as artist', 'I as scholar', 'I as learner', and so forth. Each of these voices carries emotional, ethical, and historical resonances. When these inner positions are silenced – through standardisation, surveillance, or emotional suppression – teachers experience fragmentation and alienation. Conversely, when teachers are encouraged to listen to, articulate, and integrate these voices, they can reestablish inner coherence and belonging.

The dialogical self thus reframes well-being not as equilibrium but as resonance – a capacity to sustain dialogue among conflicting positions and to find meaning in that tension (Raggatt, 2012). This interpretation resonates with recent scholarship on teacher emotional sustainability, which emphasises the importance of reflective spaces, relational trust, and narrative sense-making (Schutz et al., 2018). Teachers' emotional well-being emerges not from the absence of conflict but from their ability to navigate it dialogically.

This insight has practical implications for teacher education and professional development. Programs grounded in dialogical approaches can foster inner speech awareness (Vygotsky, 1986), narrative reflexivity, and artistic expression as pathways to well-being. As the chapters of this book demonstrate – through photography, theatre metaphors, soundscapes, and embodied inquiry – art-based and reflective practices serve as mediating tools that reconnect teachers to their inner voices. Such practices are not peripheral but essential for sustaining professional vitality. They cultivate pedagogical presence, enabling teachers to meet students, colleagues, and themselves with authenticity.

DST also challenges the deficit-oriented language often used in discussions of teacher stress. Rather than viewing teachers as lacking resilience or coping skills, a dialogical perspective recognises that conflict and vulnerability are inherent to human development. Well-being arises not from eliminating struggle but from cultivating meaning through it. In this view, teacher well-being is the ongoing art of responding dialogically to life's multiplicity.

Moving Within Learning Communities

The movement of teachers within learning communities can be understood as a series of relational and reflective enactments, through which professional well-being is actively performed. Engaging in professional networks and collaborative spaces allows these positions to enter into dialogue, fostering reflexivity, agency, and a sense of coherence across professional experiences.

Professional well-being emerges here as an act of negotiation and recognition: as teachers share experiences, exchange perspectives, and respond to challenges, they perform practices that integrate emotional, cognitive, and relational dimensions of their professional lives. Each interaction within a learning community becomes an opportunity to articulate, reposition, or affirm aspects of the self – whether as mentor, innovator, reflective practitioner, or learner. These movements are performative in that they both reveal and constitute the teacher's ongoing process of professional self-construction.

Drawing on the dialogical self, learning communities function as relational arenas where teachers can explore tensions between competing professional I-positions (e.g., efficiency vs. care, authority vs. collaboration) and reconcile them through dialogue. Well-being is thus enacted through these interactions: it is maintained and expanded not merely through external support or resources but through the internal regulation of affective and cognitive states as mediated by dialogue with others and with oneself.

Moreover, moving across multiple professional spaces – face-to-face or digital – enables teachers to experiment with new roles, gain validation, and reframe challenges as opportunities for growth. Professional well-being, in this view, is not a static attribute but a lived accomplishment, a performative process of negotiating identity, sustaining engagement, and maintaining affective equilibrium within relationally and contextually diverse environments.

In sum, moving within learning communities is an enactment of professional well-being through dialogical engagement, where teachers actively construct and perform their professional selves, integrating multiple voices, roles, and perspectives in the ongoing work of professional growth.

The movement of teachers within and between learning communities can be understood as a performative practice of professional well-being. Within this framing, professional well-being is not simply a static state (e.g., absence of stress, satisfaction) but rather a relational, enacted, and dialogical process by which professionals maintain, regenerate, and transform their professional selves. Teachers engage in different forms of professional gatherings – formal staff -meetings, collaborative planning groups, cross-institutional networks, digital interest groups. Each 'movement' (joining, contributing, leaving, shifting roles) entails a re-positioning of the self: one becomes learner, mentor, collaborator, challenger. These enactments constitute part of how teachers perform their professional selves. From this perspective, professional well -being is enacted when teachers feel competent, connected, and agentic. By participating in communities, teachers perform and affirm their capacities: they contribute ideas, exchange experiences, receive recognition, reflect upon practices. The relational dimension (connection with others) and identity dimension (who I am as teacher) come together.

Operationalising 'movement' for well-being:

- Entering a community: teacher steps into a new professional space, thereby signalling openness, readiness to learn – performing self as learner and signalling connection which supports belonging and relational well-being.
- Engaging (active participation, sharing, collaboration): teacher performs self as contributor, reinforcing self-efficacy and competence – core to well-being.
- Transitioning/Exiting: by moving out, shifting roles or reshaping involvement, teacher enacts agency, choice, change which supports autonomy and renewal of professional self.

These movements across roles and communities serve affective, cognitive and social dimensions of professional well-being.

Building on the above, consider that a teacher's movement into, within and out of learning communities (physical, virtual, hybrid) becomes a vehicle for enacting reflectivity, collaboration and agency.

- Reflective practice is stimulated when teachers join a community, articulate their questions, engage in dialogs, and then return to their classroom with new professional narratives.
- Collaborative practice is realised as teachers share, co-construct, mediate artefacts and dialogue across boundaries – a feature evident in work on epistemic collaborative communities via social networks (Baker-Doyle & Yoon, 2020; Impedovo, 2021b).
- Agency is exercised when teachers decide to join a community, negotiate their roles, shift between roles (learner, mentor, convenor), and move beyond passive participation to active professional shaping. In the master's-study, teachers expressed agency in transforming their own and collective practices.

Thus, movement across communities is not merely a change of setting or membership; it is a performative enactment of professional self-hood and well-being: by moving, teachers perform their competence, belonging and growth.

Towards a Relational and Dialogical Future of Teacher Education

Educational systems thus cultivate cultures of attentiveness – listening to teachers' voices not as data points but as expressions of lived humanity. In doing so, we move towards what Biesta (2020) calls 'the beautiful risk of education': an encounter with the other that is never fully predictable but deeply human.

Well-being, in this sense, is not an endpoint but a mode of being-with – with oneself, with others, with the profession. It is sustained when teachers can inhabit their multiplicity without fragmentation, when their inner dialogs are heard within the larger dialogs of the educational community.

Teacher well-being is not only an individual or internal matter; it is profoundly relational, emerging through engagement with colleagues and participation in professional communities. Moving within learning communities – physically, socially, and cognitively – can be understood as a form of performing well-being, in which teachers inhabit spaces that simultaneously support reflection, dialogue, and professional growth. These communities allow teachers to enact, rehearse, and negotiate their multiple professional voices – such as the teacher as mentor, learner, researcher, or advocate – within a relational setting that affirms both identity and agency.

Participation in such communities enables teachers to share experiences, exchange strategies, and collectively reflect on pedagogical challenges. This relational engagement creates conditions in which teachers' emotional and professional capacities are reinforced, providing both recognition and validation. Well-being, in this sense, is not merely an internal state but a practiced, enacted phenomenon, cultivated through repeated interactions, shared narratives, and collaborative problem-solving.

These professional communities also function as arenas for experimentation and rehearsal. Teachers can explore new practices, reimagine roles, and test different aspects of their professional selves within a supportive social space. Such enactment strengthens their sense of coherence, belonging, and resilience. Moreover, by participating in ongoing dialogue and collective reflection, teachers expand the repertoire of voices that constitute their dialogical self, fostering a richer, more integrated professional identity.

In closing, the teacher dialogical self offers a vision for education that is both profoundly personal and deeply social. It invites us to imagine professional development not as a ladder of progression but as a mosaic of encounters, each voice adding to the polyphony of what it means to teach and to be. In times when the profession is threatened by exhaustion and depersonalisation, this vision calls us back to the source: to dialogue as the heartbeat of teaching, to belonging as the foundation of well-being, and to becoming as the ongoing ethical call that sustains the teacher's presence in the world.

REFERENCES

Ana, A., Kustiawan, I., Ahman, E., Zakaria, S., Muktiarni, M., Dwiyanti, V., … Kahoerunnisa, I. (2020). Defining vocational teacher competencies in industry 4.0 from the perspective of policymakers. *Journal of Engineering Education Transformations, 34*(Special Issue).

Baker-Doyle, K. J., & Yoon, S. A. (2020). The social side of teacher education: Implications of social network research for the design of professional development. *International Journal of Educational Research, 101*, 101563.

Bakhtin, M. (1986). *Speech genres and other late essays.* University of Texas Press.

Biesta, G. (2020). *World-centred education: A view for the present.* Routledge.

Dania, A., & Impedovo, M. A. (2025). Preservice teachers' perceptions of teacher competence: The influence of national and global frameworks. *Professional Development in Education*, 1–17.

Day, C., & Gu, Q. (2010). *The new lives of teachers.* Routledge.

Day, C., & Hong, J. (2016). Influences on the capacities for emotional resilience of teachers in schools serving disadvantaged urban communities: Challenges of living on the edge. *Teaching and Teacher Education, 59*, 115–125.

Hargreaves, A., & Fullan, M. (2020). Professional capital after the pandemic: Revisiting and revising classic understandings of teachers' work. *Journal of Professional Capital and Community, 5*(3/4), 327–336.

Hermans, H. J. M., & Hermans-Konopka, A. (2010). *Dialogical self theory: Positioning and counter-positioning in a globalizing society.* Cambridge University Press.

Hermans, H. J. M. (2011). *The dialogical self: Positioning and counter-positioning in a globalizing society.* Cambridge University Press.

Impedovo, M. A. (2021a). Identity and teacher professional development: A reflective, collaborative and agentive learning journey. *SpringerBriefs in Education.* https://doi.org/10.1007/978-3-030-71367-6

Impedovo, M. A. (2021b). New forms of teacher professional development: Developing epistemic collaborative communities via social networks. *Teacher Education Advancement Network Journal, 13*(1), 66–72.

Kelchtermans, G. (2009). Who I am in how I teach is the message: Self-understanding, vulnerability and reflection. *Teachers and Teaching: Theory and Practice, 15*(2), 257–272.

Klassen, R. M., & Chiu, M. M. (2011). The occupational commitment and intention to quit of practicing and pre-service teachers. *Teaching and Teacher Education, 27*(5), 1023–1034.

OECD. (2021, 2022). *Education at a glance: OECD indicators.* OECD Publishing.

Raggatt, P. T. (2012). Positioning in the dialogical self: Recent advances in theory construction.

Ryan, R. M., & Deci, E. L. (2017). *Self-determination theory: Basic psychological needs in motivation, development, and wellness.* Guilford.

Schutz, P. A., Hong, J. Y., & Cross Francis, D. (2018). Research on teacher identity: Mapping challenges and innovations. *Educational Psychologist, 53*(1), 1–21.

Skaalvik, E. M., & Skaalvik, S. (2018). Job demands and resources as predictors of teacher motivation and well-being. *Social Psychology of Education, 21*(5), 1251–1275.

Sturrock, S. (2022). Primary teachers' experiences of neo-liberal education reform in England: 'Nothing is ever good enough'. *Research Papers in Education, 37*(6), 1214–1240.

Teachers for Education 2030 (TTF). https://teachertaskforce.org/

UNESCO. (2023). *Global report on teachers: Addressing teacher shortages and transforming the profession.* https://doi.org/10.54675/FIGU8035

Vygotsky, L. S. (1986). *Thought and language.* MIT Press.

CHAPTER 12

POINTS FOR DEBATE – WRITING OTHERWISE ON TEACHER PROFESSIONAL IDENTITY

ABSTRACT

This section explores what may unfold when academic writing intentionally departs from conventional norms. Rather than treating writing as a neutral representational tool, the approach adopted here embraces ambiguity, experimentation, and playfulness as pathways towards generating new understandings. Writing is framed as an ethical and imaginative practice that resists institutional pressures limiting creativity and narrowing scholarly inquiry. Building on this orientation, the chapter introduces a series of alternative modalities – real and fictional vignettes, artistic practices, dilemmas and journaling, metaphor, performative reflection, anecdote, chance-based exercises, and haiku – to disrupt habitual academic forms and open more expansive epistemic possibilities concerning teacher professional development. Through these creative approaches, scholarship on teacher professional identity and the teacher Self becomes a space of inquiry that is fluid, reflective, and ethically responsive. The exploration culminates in a focus on drawing the 'teacher identity island', offering a nuanced lens through which to consider how educators negotiate and inhabit their evolving professional selves.

Keywords: Academic writing; conventional norms; creative approaches; teacher professional identity; teacher self

Teacher Dialogical Self, pages 135–141

doi:10.1108/978-1-80686-957-220261013

INTRODUCTION

Academic writing often operates within well-established conventions that shape not only how knowledge is communicated but also how it is imagined. This chapter proposes a shift away from these normative boundaries by inviting forms of writing that welcome ambiguity, experimentation, and playfulness. Approaching writing as an ethical and imaginative practice, the chapter challenges institutional expectations that may constrain creativity and narrow the scope of scholarly inquiry. To explore these possibilities, a variety of alternative modalities – ranging from vignettes and artistic practices to journaling, metaphor, performative reflection, anecdote, chance-based exercises, and haiku – are mobilised to unsettle familiar academic forms. In doing so, the chapter opens new pathways for thinking about teacher professional development and the evolving teacher Self. The journey culminates in the creation of a 'teacher identity island', a conceptual and visual prompt that supports a more nuanced understanding of how educators navigate and inhabit their professional identities.

Writing Otherwise

The section tried to apply the invitation of Taylor et al. (2025): What might happen if we decide to write otherwise? The passage argues for a mode of academic writing that welcomes ambiguity, experimentation, and playfulness instead of conforming to standardized expectations. Rather than treating writing as a transparent vehicle for representation, this approach embraces its capacity to disrupt, unsettle, and generate new ways of thinking. It frames writing as an ethical and imaginative practice that resists the pressures and norms embedded in academic institutions, which often narrow creativity and diminish the vitality of thought.

Within this perspective, writing becomes a space for exploring alternative possibilities – different presents and futures for scholarship itself. The 'writing otherwise' invitation highlights how power relations, institutional histories, and systemic inequalities shape what is considered acceptable or legitimate writing. Yet it also emphasises that every writing situation holds latent transformative potential.

A wide range of creative exercises are possible in the writing otherwise: free writing, place-based writing, improvisation, visual-textual experiments, collaborative collage, and forms of writing that dispense with words or emerge spontaneously in the moment. These practices treated writing as a collective, unfolding process, where form and content evolve together.

Taylor et al. (2025) present this collaborative experimentation as a political gesture. By foregrounding embodied, affective, and situated aspects of writing, such practices can question the authority of conventional academic gatekeepers. They also reaffirm the value of co-creation, positioning shared creativity as a route towards unfamiliar, generative directions that disrupt individualistic authorship. Through these collective movements, writing becomes a site where new relational forms of knowledge can emerge and where academic futures might be reimagined.

Building on this orientation, a series of alternative modalities have been used to write about professional identity and teacher Self in the book. These limited examples are here proposed to suggest way to break away from habitual academic forms and activate more expansive ways of knowing.

- Real and fictional vignettes.
  Brief narrative scenes – whether drawn from lived experience or entirely imagined – allow writers to approach complex issues indirectly (Saldaña, 2016; Schratz et al., 2013). By concentrating meaning into a situated moment, vignettes open emotional, sensory, and relational dimensions that conventional exposition often suppresses. Fictionalised episodes, in particular, enable writers to explore the 'what if' of research, making space for intuition, uncertainty, and speculative insight.
- Use of art.
  Integrating artistic practices – sketching, collage, visual composition, sound, or embodied movement – invites a different tempo of thinking. Art activates forms of attention that are tactile, affective, and atmospheric. When writing emerges in dialogue with artistic experimentation, it tends to loosen its structural rigidity and become more receptive to nuance, contradiction, and emergent meaning.
- Dilemmas and journaling.
  Writing from a dilemma foregrounds the tensions, doubts, and ethical frictions that shape research but often remain hidden in final outputs (for an example in teacher professional development, Tan et al., 2015). Journaling deepens this stance by capturing the unfolding of thought in real time. Both forms allow writers to inhabit their uncertainties rather than prematurely resolving them, emphasising writing as a process of inquiry rather than demonstration.
- Metaphor.
  Metaphorical writing helps shift attention from fixed definitions to relational thinking. Metaphors work by connecting disparate domains, generating fresh associations and revealing unnoticed dynamics. They can hold complexity without reducing it, offering writers a way to think with images, sensations, and affective resonances.

- Performative reflection and inner speech.
  Writing that stages its own coming-into-being – through dialogs with the self, stream-of-consciousness, or embodied voice – disrupts the illusion of neutral, disembodied authorship. Inner speech highlights the hesitations, impulses, and micro-movements of thinking (Fossa, 2022). Performative reflection makes the act of writing visible, turning the page into a site where cognition, emotion, and gesture intertwine.
- Anecdote.
  Short, personal stories illuminate how theory touches lived experience (Doecke et al., 2000). Anecdotes can reveal the situatedness of knowledge, highlighting the everyday textures of academic life. When used critically, they destabilise hierarchical divisions between 'data' and 'life', and open scholarship to forms of insight that are modest, intimate, and deeply contextual.
- Dice game.
  Introducing chance through simple tools – like rolling dice to select topics, perspectives, or constraints – can displace entrenched habits and encourage surprize. Random prompts push writers into unfamiliar trajectories, fostering playfulness and experimentation. Chance-based methods help disrupt the drive towards control and predetermined outcomes that often characterises academic writing.
- Heiko.
  This concise poetic form, with its attention to brevity, rhythm, and atmosphere, trains writers to distill meaning into minimal strokes. Haiku-like approaches encourage sensitivity to the moment, an attunement to detail, and an acceptance of incompleteness. Such practices foreground the evocative power of the unsaid and invite writing to breathe rather than explain.

  Taken together, these modalities are limitated example in the tentative of broaden what academic writing can do. Each one shifts attention towards relationality, atmosphere, affect, embodiment, and co-creation. By experimenting with them, writers begin to inhabit scholarship about teacher Self as a creative, situated, and ethically attentive practice – one capable of imagining different academic presents and futures.

Teacher Identity Isle

To extend this creative exploration, I concentrate on a single small island within Macfarlane's (2012) original 'Higher Education Research Archipelago': the island of teacher identity (see Fig. 6). This focused lens allows me to delve more deeply into the shifting contours of how educators understand, negotiate, and inhabit their professional selves.

Fig. 6. Identity Isle Inspired by Macfarlane's (2012).

This vignette below offers a reflective journey into the evolving landscape of teacher identity, drawn from my own experiences as a teacher educator and researcher. It illustrates how professional identities are not fixed, but continually negotiated across intersecting roles, moments, and contexts. Using the metaphor of an island, the narrative visualises the shifting, sometimes capricious nature of the teacher Self, emphasising the interplay of reflection, emotion, and embodiment.

Vignette

Ever since I stumbled into teacher education research as a young academic in 2014, when I first arrived at the School of Education, I have been trying to grasp what we mean when we speak of 'teacher identity' – at the same time as my own identity as a teacher educator was beginning to take shape. My professional path – beginning in work psychology and later unfolding into my role as an associate professor in higher education – has offered me multiple vantage points from which to observe how this identity is formed, negotiated, and lived by teacher-students and teachers in service, as well as by myself as a teacher educator.

Inspired by explorations of imaginative academic cartographies I recently discovered, I sketch teacher identity here as an island – a shifting and sometimes capricious territory where different elements continually reshape the landscape, a theoretical abstraction of concepts visualised on the page.

This small disegno invites not merely observing from afar – I am navigating it, sometimes confidently, sometimes hesitantly, always aware that the ground beneath me is alive and, in some way, unknown, since every educator and teacher inhabits their identity space in a unique manner.

Observing my own identity space as a teacher, I can see how it is inhabited by multiple, intersecting positions at once, and how a fleeting moment – a gesture, a hesitation, a smile that fades too quickly – reveals more than any formal definition. I find myself listening to the soft undercurrent of my inner speech, those whispered negotiations between different positions. At times, I am guided by the subtle pull of bodily and emotional states, those hidden tides that shape presence long before words arrive.

There are days when the island slows me down, urging me to notice the rhythm between action and reflection, the pauses that carry as much meaning as the movement. And always, I return to the evolving sense of role and presence that I craft – sometimes deliberately, sometimes by accident – as I move through new professional horizons.

Walking this island as a researcher feels less like mapping a territory and more like accompanying its transformations. Each turn reveals a new contour, a shift in light, an unexpected trace of what it means to become a teacher. And so I keep exploring, knowing that the island will never fully settle – and that its very restlessness is what makes the journey worthwhile.

I share this small 'map' as a light-hearted extension of previous creative attempts to imagine the terrain of academic life. It is not meant to be read with excessive seriousness; its purpose is partly playful, partly reflective. If we accept that our understandings of teaching and learning are shaped in dialogue with our contexts – and that the grand, universal explanations of the past have long since drifted out of reach – then it is only natural that each of us would draw this landscape differently.

I stroll through its contours as teacher and researcher, linger over its details, and reflect on how identity constantly shifts and takes form in the ordinary, often unnoticed movements of daily practice.

By attending to subtle gestures, fleeting moments, and inner dialogs, the vignette invites readers to consider identity as lived and relational rather than abstract or static. Positioned within the broader exploration of creative academic writing, this narrative exemplifies how personal, imaginative, and situated forms of inquiry can illuminate the complexities of professional development, providing both researchers and teachers with tools to navigate, interpret, and reimagine the contours of teaching practice.

CONCLUSION

In stepping beyond conventional academic forms, this chapter has illustrated how creative modalities can expand the ways we explore teacher identity and professional development. Engaging with fiction, artmaking, metaphor, journaling, performative reflection, and chance-based practices demonstrates that inquiry need not be confined to linear analysis or representational clarity. For the researcher, these approaches cultivate openness to the unexpected, allowing new questions, sensibilities, and interpretive pathways to emerge. Creativity thus becomes not an embellishment but a methodological resource – one that supports more situated, affective, and ethically attuned understandings of the teacher Self.

For teachers, the same creative stance offers opportunities to reimagine their professional identities as dynamic, relational, and continually in formation. By attending to ambiguity, emotion, and embodied experience, educators can approach their professional growth not as a fixed trajectory but as an ongoing process of becoming. These explorations highlight the generative power of writing and reflection as tools for self-understanding and pedagogical renewal. Ultimately, fostering creativity in both research and practice encourages more expansive, responsive, and humane orientations to the complex work of teaching.

REFERENCES

Doecke, B., Brown, J., & Loughran, J. (2000). Teacher talk: The role of story and anecdote in constructing professional knowledge for beginning teachers. *Teaching and Teacher Education, 16*(3), 335–348.

Fossa, P. (Ed.). (2022). *New perspectives on inner speech* (pp. 65–80). Springer.

Macfarlane, B. (2012). The higher education research archipelago. *Higher Education Research and Development, 31*(1), 129–131. https://doi.org/10.1080/07294360.2012.642846

Saldaña, J. (2016). *Ethnotheatre: Research from page to stage.* Routledge.

Schratz, M., Schwarz, J. F., & Westfall-Greiter, T. (2013). Looking at two sides of the same coin: Phenomenologically oriented vignette research and its implications for teaching and learning. *Studia paedagogica, 18*(4), 57–73.

Tan, A. L., Chang, C. H., & Teng, P. (2015). Tensions and dilemmas in teacher professional development. *Procedia-Social and Behavioral Sciences, 174,* 1583–1591.

Taylor, C. A., Benozzo, A., Fairchild, N., Pihkala, S., & Cranham, J. (2025). Academic writing otherwise: Possibilities and praxis. *Qualitative Inquiry,* 10778004251337410.

www.ingramcontent.com/pod-product-compliance
Lightning Source LLC
LaVergne TN
LVHW021604090826
845264LV00025B/365
* 9 7 8 1 8 0 6 8 6 9 6 0 2 *